THE PRE-ADAMITE,

OR

WHO TEMPTED EVE?

1. Mongolian. 2. Malay.
3. Caucasian. 4. Negro.
5. American Indian.

THE PRE-ADAMITE,

OR

WHO TEMPTED EVE?

SCRIPTURE AND SCIENCE IN UNISON AS RESPECTS THE ANTIQUITY OF MAN.

By A. HOYLE LESTER.

Let Wisdom with all her science trace
Mankind of yore, and where begins the race,
Where born, and when; let all his traits appear,
His history solve, through each revolving year.

PHILADELPHIA:
PUBLISHED FOR THE AUTHOR BY
J. B. LIPPINCOTT & CO.
1875.

THIS WORK

IS RESPECTFULLY DEDICATED

TO MY WORTHY FRIEND,

DR. T. J. DRANE,

WITHOUT HIS KNOWLEDGE OR CONSENT;

AND THE OFFERING IS SIMPLY A TESTIMONIAL OF THE KINDLY FEELINGS ENTERTAINED FOR HIM

BY THE AUTHOR,

A. HOYLE LESTER.

TO THE READER.

FOR convenience of reference, I deem it necessary to insert a Chronological Table, which gives the computations of various parties who have devoted much time to this subject, which is denominated the short, or received chronology, and the long chronology, which gives the dates of the principal periods from the creation of the world to the birth of Christ.

CHRONOLOGICAL TABLE.

	SHORT SYSTEM.			LONG SYSTEM.		
	Ussher.	Petavius.	Clinton.	Hales.	Jackson.	Poole.
	B.C.	B.C.	B.C.	B.C.	B.C.	B.C.
Creation	4004	3983	4138	5411	5426	5421
Flood	2349	2327	2482	3155	3170	3159
Call of Abraham	1921	1961	2055	2078	2023	2082
Exodus	1491	1531	1625	1648	1593	1652
Foundation of Temple	1012	1012	1013	1027	1014	1010
Destruction of Temple	588	589	587	586	586	586

Archbishop Ussher's computation, as above, has been universally adopted, as found in the margin of the authorized English version of the Bible.

And for the satisfaction of those who take an interest in the ancient history of Egypt, and who may wish to refer to the pyramidal period of the old empire, I have concluded to insert Manetho's system of Egyptian chronology. Many of the ante-historical dynasties are omitted, when the Egyptians claimed to be ruled over by gods and demigods; and we will begin at the epoch of Menes, or Man, which is the commencement of the historical period of the thirty dynasties.

First Dynasty.—Accession of Menes, began 3893 B.C.

Third Dynasty.—Commenced the monumental period.

Fourth Dynasty.—Pyramids and tombs extant, began 3426 B.C.

Fifth Dynasty.—Began about 3100 B.C.

Seventh Dynasty.—Began about 2900 B.C.

Tenth Dynasty.—Began about 2500 B.C.

Twelfth Dynasty.—Ends about 2124 B.C.

Thirteenth Dynasty.—Ends about 2100 B.C.

Fourteenth, Fifteenth, Sixteenth Dynasty.—Hyksos, or shepherd kings, from 2000 B.C. to 1590 B.C.

The new empire or restoration succeeds:

Seventeenth Dynasty.—Began 1671 B.C.

Thirtieth Dynasty.—Ends on second Persian invasion, 340 B.C.

Egypt conquered by Alexander, 332 B.C.

Ptolemaic Dynasty.—Began 323 B.C.

Ptolemaic Dynasty.—Ends 44 B.C.

Roman Dynasty.—Began 30 B.C.

PREFACE.

THE intellect of man is progressive, and cannot remain stationary while science marks out the line of progress, and Revelation does not forbid our going forward in the work of investigation.

That the earth is much older than our wisest sages were once willing to admit is a fact which science reveals to us almost daily, and which the theologian unites with us in establishing in a way not at variance with Divine revelation.

The Bible and Science move together harmoniously, and where there are seeming inconsistencies there can be no controversy. Our interpretation of Scripture is either incorrect and needs modification to place it in harmony with the progress of Science, or else the scientist has failed in his deductions, and presents a dogma which has an existence only in theory and not in fact.

Who believed fifty years ago that the lightnings of heaven would be used to transmit our messages from zone to zone, and from the sea to the uttermost parts of the earth? And yet Job declares, in chap. xxxviii. 35, "Canst thou send lightnings, that they may go, and say unto thee, Here we are?" The same may be said in regard to the powers of steam, when Job describes Leviathan as emitting flames from his nostrils and plowing the vasty deep, until his pathway becomes hoary with phosphorescent light. Science reveals to us the revolutions of all the planets upon their axes, and a myriad of worlds beyond our own system. Gen. i. 4, 5: "And God divided the light from the darkness. And God called the light Day, and the darkness he called Night." There is no want of harmony in all this, and yet how slow was the Christian world in adopting this new system of astronomy!

The unity of the human race is comparatively a new theory, which has been strongly maintained by the translators of the English version of the Bible. However, the ancient world, and the Jews particularly, believed firmly in the diversity of the human family; and all nations under the sun, and in every age, who have held intercourse with the dark races, have regarded them as distinct in character, and as constituting intellectually an inferior type of the genus homo.

A. H. L.

CONTENTS.

THE PRE-ADAMITE.

CHAPTER I.

ADAM NOT THE FIRST MAN.

"Together let us beat this ample field;
Try what the open, what the covert yield;
The latent tracks, the giddy heights explore,
Of all who blindly creep or sightless soar."—POPE.

THAT the enlightened mind of the nineteenth century can content itself with the theory that the Chinese, the Indian, and the Negro descended from the same original progenitor is the source of no great astonishment to the thinking man of the present age, as the love of ease and the cherished opinions of the past are ever marked with foot-prints dear to the memory of man, consequently he is indisposed to permit innovations within the precincts of his established views.

That Adam was not the father of the above-mentioned races, and was only the ancestor of the Caucasian family, I am heartily convinced can be established by sound reasoning and good, practical sense, and at the same time on a basis not at all antagonistic to the revelations of Holy Writ.

This generation remembers when able theologians contended that the world had only been created about six thousand years, and that the creation had been perfected by the Almighty in six days of the ordinary duration of twenty-four hours. The investigations of science have exploded this hypothesis, and no person now, who makes any pretensions to scientific lore, would stake his reputation in combating a dogma so thoroughly fixed in the human mind.

In opening the bowels of the earth, we trace its history in the various formations through which we pass, and in the peculiar texture of the various deposits which we find imbedded beneath its surface. And thus, like the man of science in mastering the organism of the human frame, he becomes familiar with its peculiarities, and tells us its comparative age, and the sex to which it belongs; and so with the various races which God in his wisdom, and at sundry times, has placed on this sublunary sphere. It behooves us to investigate their history, their traits of character, and their origin.

CHAPTER II.

THE ORDER OF CREATION.

> "So from the first eternal order ran,
> And creature linked to creature, man to man."—POPE.

THE world when it was first fashioned by the plastic hand of Jehovah was a barren waste, void and without form, and darkness was upon the face of the deep. Matter assumed shape; atmosphere, with its vivifying influences, took wing and sought its equilibrium throughout the immensity of space; waters were formed and sought their level in the low basins of the earth; hence lakes, seas, and oceans. And light, by the fiat of the Almighty, sprang out from the hidden caverns of immensity, and shot its rays like the fiery chain that springs from the bosom of the electrified cloud, and swept across the face of a new-born world, and infused animation into the unproductive elements of nature. Day came and went, and the dew and the shower united together, and performed their commissioned duties, to give life and invigorate the germ which the creative genius of Deity had planted in the vast fields which He had recently formed.

The grass, the herb, the tree, sprang into life, bloomed and shed its fragrance upon the desert air, and ripened its fruit at the new-appointed harvest. The waters were moved by the creative hand of Deity, and the river and the ocean became alive with the animalculæ and the leviathan. Birds winged their rapid flight through the yielding atmosphere, and fed upon the varied insects that peopled the luxuriant fields, and sang their morning song and their evening lullaby where their warbling notes as yet fell upon no mortal ear.

In the course of many ages the surface of this earth had parted with its heat, and the active influences of dews and showers had prepared many portions of the world for the growth and maturity of plants; and no doubt in the lapse of time vast plains were covered with luxuriant verdure, while other sections were sterile and parched by a meridian sun, and desolated by the scorching fires of active volcanoes. On these fertile plains and prolific slopes, where verdant pastures and flowing brooks could support animal life, God there placed the lower order of the animal creation, until times and seasons had passed over the face of nature, and prepared a habitation for the maintenance of a higher order of animal existence. So on thus, from one gradation to another, did He in his wisdom modify and reconstruct by the gradual growth and decomposition of the vegetable kingdom, until the lion, the tiger, and the horse, the highest order of the brute creation, could move and have their being, amid the forests and jungles of a world which had never as yet echoed to the voice of man.

In the ascending series of the creative programme comes the monkey, or the lower grade of the quadrumana tribes, and in due course of formation we have the baboon and the orang-outang, who occupy their periods in the creative designs of the Great I Am, until finally the gorilla, the highest standard of the quadrumana race, takes his position among created animals, and forms the uniting link between the brute creation and the lowest standard of the human family.

Ages upon ages, in all probability, had rolled over this mundane sphere since first it was thrown out in a molten state to find its regular orbit, and assume shape in winging its trackless flight along the unmeasured paths of immensity, and in fancied dreams we can still behold it blazing like a fiery comet when approaching its perihelion. We may well assume, as respects this world at the age of which we write, that the atmosphere which encircled it was impregnated with the heat arising from internal fires, consequently unfitted for the abode of Adam's race, of whom we shall speak in due time. In the crude and unsublimated condition of the world at this epoch, God saw proper to place a pair of human beings on our orb, and invested them with full possession, with all the rights and privileges of the first occupants. He endowed them with speech and with a higher degree of intelligence than that bestowed upon any animal of a former creation; He gave them laws and rules and regulations by which they should be governed, and demanded of them obedience in accordance with his divine behest, and sent them forth to multiply and people the untrodden labyrinths of earth. This was the negro, and his native land, Africa; the same whom the Anglo-Saxon introduced upon the American continent, and wherever found to-day in his ancestral clime, and whose blood is still unalloyed with the refining influences of a nobler and a higher race, we trace in him all the savage instincts that mark the very beasts that walk the earth. He served his period under the benign sway of Divine Providence; fell from his high estate, and was permitted to wander adrift, and gratify the unholy passions prompted by his unholy nature. Anthropophagi, he preyed upon his fellow-man; he sinned away his day of grace, and his kind Benefactor permitted him to become a reprobate, given over to a hardness of heart and a reprobation of mind, that he might believe a lie and be lost.

I stated in the beginning of this discourse that the theory advanced herein in reference to a diversity in the origin of the human races should in nowise conflict with the teachings of Revelation.

I assume this position: That in the progress of creation and through its various periods, as God saw that the earth, the air, and the water were adapted to the growth and nourishment of the different species with which, in his divine economy, He proposed to people these elements, and age after age, as these necessary changes would take place, He did form and create all the peculiar animal life which has ever existed on this globe; not in one day, or in one period, but in different epochs, and in accordance as He saw that these essential changes in nature required nobler creations. Thus He first formed the zoophyte and the lower animals, with every creeping thing, and so on in their regular order, until this world became a suitable abode for the lowest caste of the human family.

The negro was introduced and became the sole occupant of this vast territory. He was created black the better to enable him to endure the intolerable heat to which the world was subjected at this period, and at no time since has he desired to emigrate from the tropical clime which he has inhabited from the first hour of his introduction.

I further assume that the next creation of a higher order was the Malay, also an inhabitant of the tropics; and after the Malay in due course comes the American Indian, and still in after-periods, but in regular order, we have the Chinese, or rather the Turanian family. Each race in its turn having a distinct origin, and in no way connected with any former creation, further than that an all-wise Providence is the creator of us all, whom all admit He can create and can destroy.

And last but not least, God in his wisdom and *in his own image* created He male and female, Adam and Eve, the progenitors of the Caucasian race. In each successive race, from the flat-nosed and woolly-headed African to the highest type of divine creation, we are compelled to admit that the intellectual elements in each develop themselves in the same ratio as we leave the negro and approach the white man. History proves this assertion, which will be alluded to in its proper place. I shall also speak of the peculiar traits of character, habits, manners, and physical formation of these respective races.

CHAPTER III.

WHO TEMPTED EVE?

"Say first of God above, or man below,
What can we reason but from what we know;
Of man what see we but his station here,
From which to reason or to which refer."

It is highly probable that there may have existed a dozen or more distinct races of the genus homo, and they may be in existence now! Still, it answers our purpose to recognize only five races, as this subdivision has already been made, and is sanctioned by ethnologists of our age. They have, however, almost universally been traced back to the same ancestor, under a belief of the unity of the races, which theory attaches itself like an incubus to the fair Caucasian, and brings a blush to the cheek of intelligent beauty. I would wipe this stain from our escutcheon, and set at right the inquiring mind, as regards the error in question.

Let not the Bible reader or the orthodox Christian cry out *skeptic*, should the author attack erroneous notions entertained by them as respects the early history of the world, and how the African and the Turanian crossed the destroying flood that wafted Noah's heavily-freighted ark to the mountains of Ararat.

I promised the attentive reader to handle this subject in the spirit of kindness, and would ask him or her to divest the mind of any prejudicial views entertained on this interesting question. Josephus, the great uninspired Jewish writer, tells us that Adam* was a red man, being formed of red clay, which was the purest of earth, as though he would convey the idea to posterity that the progenitor of his race was made of no common material, and in fact of better material than any prior creation. Before the time of Moses the only history of the world that existed was traditional, and was handed down from sire to son; and by this channel, together with his acquaintance with the original Hebrew, the Jewish scribe was enabled to communicate this information to those whose opportunities were not so good for acquiring knowledge of ancient history. He was named Adam because he was red, of a ruddy countenance. He was the father of the blushing race. Created He him in his own image and likeness. The only immortal soul beneath the wide-expanded canopy of heaven to whose cheeks gushed the crimson blood to manifest the intense shame of conscious guilt! and if the darker races blush, with whom we claim no kindred blood, then, like the wild-flower in its native wilderness, it blushes unseen and wastes its virtue on the desert air. The side of Adam gave birth to Eve, the mother of all living; and she, the fairest queen that ever graced the

---

* This man was called Adam, which, in the Hebrew tongue, signifies one that is red, because he was formed out of red earth, for of that kind is virgin and true earth.—*Antiq. of Jews*, page 2.

courts of earth, made her *début* on the arena of life in the romantic shades of Eden, where the creeping vine threw its tendrils around the giant oak, and lovely flowers bloomed by murmuring waters in their flow to the turbid Euphrates, and where the gentle zephyr fanned her cheek and wafted the odorous sweets from nature's untrodden plains. It is not strange that Eden's garden bird should have become wearied with the monotony that daily surrounded her. The scenery had become stale to her accustomed eye, and ceased to afford its wonted pleasure. The presence of Adam had no doubt become irksome, and his voice, for the time, had ceased to fill the aching void that agonized her tender heart; and with a desire to explore the farther limit of her terrestrial domain, she wandered far along meandering brooks, and plucked strange flowers to while away the slow-fleeting moments, and slaked her thirst at gushing fountains where she dreamed no mortal had yet partaken thereof. Imagine her surprise; innocent and unsuspecting, she meets a stranger, the serpent who had beheld her beauty (for Eve, at this unlucky hour, was not arrayed in the habiliments of modern style). She felt lonely, and was surprised to meet this handsome stranger amidst the solitudes of Eden's bower. Knowing little of this world save her own innocence, and unaware of the great gulf that lay between God and the fallen races that preceded her, she listened with attentive ear to the enchanting conversation of this son of perdition. He belonged most assuredly to the highest order of the inferior races, around whom our heavenly Father had thrown the benign influences of his exalted nature, and had offered time and again to make them sons and priests unto God, and they rejected the proffered mercy; and in the same language, we may reasonably presume, he addressed those idolaters, as he did in after-years address a more enlightened and favored people, when He declared, "O Jerusalem, Jerusalem, how often would I have gathered thy children together, even as a hen gathereth her chickens under her wings, and ye would not!"

Who was this serpent that beguiled our first parents? In our language it could not be the snake, or the viper, that besets our pathway and strikes into our flesh the fangs that bring death by the venom infused into the system. By no means! Does the adder speak, or does the boa-constrictor give utterance to language? Preposterous thought! The fall of man as revealed to us in Genesis is no metaphor. Consider, kind reader, a venomous reptile approaching a lovely maiden, to hold gentle converse in the silent wood: would she take the accursed reptile to her bosom and associate with him day after day and week after week? Never! even though his hissing voice had the melody of the enchanting siren. His shape and his demeanor in aping a deceiver would carry with it the nauseating venom, at which the native modesty and timidity of the first Caucasian damsel would have revolted, and she, like the affrighted hare before its pursuers, would have fled from its presence, and sought refuge under the protecting ægis of her Lord. Then tell us not that the devil approached our first mother in the form of a snake, as seen in the so-called sacred pictures of the passing age.

But he did present himself to Eve in the form and likeness of a man, one of Mongolia's* comeliest sons. He came possessed of all the attributes of the evil genius of perdition, clothed from head to heel with the accumulated curses of an avenging God. He was an idolater, and had no pleasure in the service of his Creator, and there was but one pair in existence at that time who were altogether innocent, and meekly trusted in the promises made to them by the Great First Cause, and that pair was our first parents; and are we surprised at the malignity and duplicity practiced upon those innocent victims, when we reflect that in this impostor was concentrated the vile essence of accumulated guilt which had been increasing in intensity, and was now ready to culminate and throw its pall of darkness over the fair race so recently ushered into existence? Lest the reader may think it unimportant, and not refer to the passages alluded to, I will quote verbatim, Matt. xxiii. 33: "Ye serpents, ye generation of vipers, how can ye escape the damnation of hell?" We here observe that serpents are applied to individuals, as of old to the Mongolian, the party who addressed Eve in her rambles amid the embowered shades of her rural paradise. He came from his ambush with the venom of the fiery serpent; with manly form, stately and erect; with that suavity of manner which age and experience had perfected, and with the wily paraphernalia which the adroit expert

* Mongolia. A country of Asia and a part of the Chinese Empire; not far distant from the garden of Eden. Mongolian, one of the divisions of mankind, and belonging properly to the Turanian family, of whom we shall speak more at length in its proper place.

puts on when he proposes to throttle his unsuspecting victim. They met often and lingered long in some solitary shade by rural founts, where human eye could not detect or make afraid. And this gay deceiver spoke of the germ in the human heart where affection springs, and of "the daughters of men that they were fair," and of love with its operations on the tender heart, and said, Partake of the forbidden fruit: "Then shall your eyes be opened, and ye shall be as gods, knowing good and evil."

Eve, poor woman, yielded to the evil machinations of this seductive deceiver. She rose from the mossy couch a wiser but a fallen creature, and returned to the presence of her lawful companion disrobed of virtue, that precious jewel, the brightest ornament of her sex.* Gen. iii. 5: "Ye shall be as gods." This Mongolian, in tempting Eve, used these words, from the fact that in every land where idolatry is the prevailing religion, we find the depraved heart bowing down and serving graven images, representing gods which are formed and fashioned after the unholy passions of the worshipers themselves, whom they endow with imaginary wisdom and power and greatness far superior to that possessed by mortal man; and from

---

* Milton, in his "Paradise Lost," in describing the effect of the forbidden fruit upon our first parents, says:

"But that false fruit
For other operation first displayed,
Carnal desire inflaming; he on Eve
Began to cast lascivious eye, she him
As wantonly repaid; in lust they burn:
Till Adam thus 'gan Eve to dalliance move."

the exuberance of his heart he expressed these views to his attentive victim. These were the gods to whom he had reference, ever forgetful of the only true and living God, who is creator of all.

From this intercourse or intimacy that subsisted between this son of perdition and the fair consort of Adam arose the mongrel offspring who bears in the Bible record the name of Cain, the vile monster who watered the earth with the blood of his brother Abel. View him as the descendant of the Asiatic nomad or pre-adamite, and we are not surprised that his offering was rejected by the Lord, or that the inherent instincts of his nature should find vent in the life-blood of so near a relative; and, in consequence of this deed, the vengeance of high heaven was visited upon this fratricide.

Gen. iv. 13–17: "And Cain said unto the Lord, My punishment is greater than I can bear. Behold, thou hast driven me out this day from the face of the earth; and from thy face shall I be hid; and I shall be a fugitive and a vagabond in the earth; and it shall come to pass, *that every one that findeth me shall slay me.* And the Lord said unto him, Therefore whosoever slayeth Cain, vengeance shall be taken on him sevenfold. And the Lord set a mark upon Cain, lest any finding him should kill him. And Cain went out from the presence of the Lord, and dwelt in the land of Nod, on the east of Eden. And Cain knew his wife; and she conceived, and bare Enoch." Why did Cain fear that he should be regarded as a fugitive and a vagabond? and whom did he apprehend would find him and slay him? Certainly not his father and mother. He had just murdered his only brother, which revelation admits. "And the Lord set a mark upon Cain, lest any finding him should kill him." Tell me, reflective reader, whom did God seem to apprehend might slay this murderer, that He would desire to place a mark upon him to shield him from the avenger of blood?

We can but admit that the world was peopled at that time by races of men which had existed long anterior to the Adamic age. Adam discovered this to his sorrow just before his expulsion from the garden of Eden, when his wife came trembling and weeping from the shady retreat, where but recently she had embraced one of the apostate sons of this sin-cursed earth. Cain and Abel had grown up in the same latitude, and had made the acquaintance of the various tribes by whom they were surrounded. Abel seems to have shunned this people, and regarded them as unworthy associates. Like an honest youth in a corrupt community, he tended his flock and brought his annual tribute as an offering to the Lord, while Cain himself cultivated their acquaintance, until his entire soul had become so demoralized that he was ready to stain his hands in the blood of an unoffending brother; and now that the deed was done, remorse hangs so heavy upon his conscience that Heaven itself must come to his rescue and brand him with a mark of guilt, so that he might return in safety to the olive-colored hordes of the East, with whom he had affiliated for years.

"And Cain went out from the presence of the Lord, and dwelt on the east of Eden." He left behind him the ordinances of God and the society of his worshipers, and the places memorable for the tokens of his divine presence. He went as an exile, and sought a home among a class of people whose feelings, habits, and sentiments were congenial, and took unto himself a wife, one of the corrupt daughters of this inferior race.

CHAPTER IV.

MISCEGENATION AND ITS ATTENDANT EVILS.

> "Force first made conquest, and that conquest law,
> Till superstition taught the tyrant awe,
> Then shar'd the tyranny, then lent it aid,
> And gods of conquerors, slaves of subjects made."
>
> POPE.

JOSEPHUS,* in speaking of Cain, says, "However, Cain did not accept of his punishment in order to amendment, but to increase his wickedness; for he only aimed to procure everything that was for his own bodily pleasure, though it obliged him to be injurious to his neighbors. He augmented his household substance with much wealth by *rapine and violence:* he excited his acquaintance to procure pleasure and spoils by robbery, and became a great leader of men into wicked courses. He also introduced a change in that way of simplicity wherein men lived before, and was the author of measures and weights; and whereas they lived innocently and generously while they knew

---

* Antiquity of the Jews, chapter ii.

nothing of such arts, he changed the world into cunning craftiness."

Can we further doubt a plurality of the races? Whether Josephus held to this view or not, he has certainly testified very pointedly in behalf of our position when he says that Cain, by plunder, rapine, and violence, was obliged to be injurious to his neighbors, and excited his acquaintance to procure pleasure and spoils by robbery. Fellow-inquirer, whom did he rob and spoil and plunder? What caste and character of neighbors were those whom he kukluxed? None others save those original tribes which had been planted on God's footstool, long ages before Eve's first-born emigrated to the land of Nod. He became a great leader of men into wicked courses. Cain was separated from his father's people; there was no intercourse whatever between the descendants of Seth and this God-forsaken wretch, who had been driven forth as a fugitive and a vagabond.

He therefore allied himself to the pre-existing generation of vipers, assumed their leadership; being of an artful turn of mind, and endowed with higher intellectual powers, he preyed upon their substance and moulded them obedient to his will, and, if it were possible, led them on still further in the baser labyrinths of recklessness and iniquity. If the reader is skeptical in regard to the conclusion just drawn, then he is referred to Gen. iv. 23: "And Lamech (a descendant of Cain) said unto his wives, Adah and Zillah, Hear my voice; ye wives of Lamech, hearken unto my speech: for I have slain a man to my wounding, and a young man to my hurt."

In illustration we find that Lamech was not only a

murderer, but was the first who inaugurated that system of free-love, or plurality of wives, which, in our day, flourishes under the name of Mormonism, borrowed no doubt from the associations around him, and which is still practiced by all those ancient races still distinct in their nature, origin, and physical formation, and denominated by geographers as Asiatic, American, Malay, and African.

Reverting to the fourth chapter of Genesis and part of the last verse, "Then began men to call upon the name of the Lord," indicates that the evil genius possessed by the pre-adamite family had infused itself into the heart of Adam's own household, to so great a degree at least that his children had ceased to reverence Jehovah, and had gone abroad amid the groves and mountains to worship the gods of these ancient idolaters, and had in the blindness of their hearts attempted to appease those deities by sacrificing on their unholy altars. But at this juncture it seems that there was a returning sense of duty, which stole over their obdurate hearts, and men again began to call on the name of the Lord. This was about the time that Noah, the great preacher of righteousness, commenced hurling anathemas against the inhabitants of earth, and threatened them with the destroying flood unless they would repent and turn from their evil ways. This brought them to reflect upon their idolatrous course, and in the anguish of their hearts they commenced to call on the name of Jehovah, and, alarmed at the impending destruction, we find that a few only of Adam's progeny were permitted to take a through passage in the vessel of that bold navigator.

Gen. vi. 1–4: "And it came to pass, when men began to multiply on the face of the earth, and daughters were born unto them, that the sons of God saw the daughters of men that they were fair; and they took them wives of all which they chose. . . . . . There were giants in the earth in those days; and also after that, when the sons of God came in unto the daughters of men, and they bare children to them, the same became mighty men which were of old, men of renown."

The sons of God intermarried among the daughters of men. This may look strange under the old régime of public opinion, but its ambiguity vanishes when we recall the fact that the sons of God were the children of Adam, and the daughters of men were the offspring of the Mongolian and the cross of Cain with the aborigines of the country. "They were fair," that is, fair to look upon, possessing figure and feature attractive to the eye, as did Pocahontas appear to John Rolfe, and the ravishing charms of Cleopatra to the lascivious eyes of Julius Cæsar and Mark Antony.

The sons of God were also those who were the true worshipers of Deity, having thus far kept aloof from the baleful influences of these original and hybrid races which "had become altogether incapable of answering the great end of divine creation." Job ii. 1: "Again there was a day when the sons of God came to present themselves before the Lord, and Satan came also among them to present himself before the Lord."

And in the form of such a disguise appears before us at this latter day the strange doctrines advanced by those who preached a higher law dogma of intellectual, political, and social equality; the former of which can never exist except in theory until Heaven's fiat is revoked, which has gone forth and stamped on the brow of the Caucasian the force of mind, of courage, and of genius, which has ever obtained in every climate and in every land where destiny has fixed his image, and social equality can only be accomplished at the sacrifice of the high moral standard which elevates our being, and the loss of which depresses the measure of our worth to the baser instincts of the savage. And the idea is forcibly and aptly illustrated in the language of the day, "that the instincts of our nature revolt at the outstincts of the negro." We here see the great sin of Adam's misguided posterity, in cohabiting with and mingling their blood with those debased aboriginal races. Through every age and in every climate, where the Caucasian has violated this great law of heaven by intermarrying with these degraded and inferior classes of people, he is reducing the high standard of intellectuality, and harnessing upon enlightened civilization a base stock of mongrels, whom experience teaches are a weak and enervated cross, and utterly debased in character, sentiment, and practice. Nor is this the only evil perpetrated upon the human family by the abominable practice of miscegenation. Heaven's vengeance comes upon us as with the besom of destruction, in that the fair fields that once blossomed as the rose have grown up in bush and brier, and the bright sunshine of prosperity is eclipsed by the dark pall that hangs over our once happy country.

It is to be hoped that no similar retribution befalls us as Heaven's vengeance thrust upon the antediluvians when Noah and his party sought refuge in the ark of safety.

"There were giants in the earth in those days; and also after that, when the sons of God came in unto the daughters of men, and they bare children to them, the same became mighty men which were of old, men of renown." There were giants in the earth in those days prior to the intermarriage of the sons of God and the daughters of men; and if so, from whom did they descend? Their progenitors certainly must have been of an earlier stock and different from our first parents. "And also after that," when the daughters of men bore children for the sons of God, showing very pointedly that the offspring by amalgamation were also giants, "which were of old, men of renown." And why were they regarded by the inspired historian as men of renown? Because they had of old become conspicuous as leaders and chieftains in the deadly warfare waged for spoil and plunder, and as nations do now when the conflict rages for supremacy and power.

And God proclaimed in language that cannot be misunderstood, "that my spirit shall not always strive with man."* And again, "I will destroy man (the Adamite) whom I have created from the face of the earth."† It is forcibly presented why God would destroy this people, because of the amalgamation of the races. This intercourse and intermixing of blood had introduced among the Adamites the interdicted worship and idolatrous devotions and damnable heresies of these debased races, who are never denominated

---

* Gen. vi. 3.

† Gen. vi. 7.

man by the inspired writer, and are only occasionally mentioned in sacred revelation, and then he is called the serpent, or the beast; the despised creature that beguiled our mother Eve, and who continued to delude and deceive the antediluvian race by engrafting upon them the forbidden practices of their own corrupt natures, until the flood came and did its work of destruction.

CHAPTER V.

THE DELUGE AND ITS TRADITION.

> "Now the thickened sky
> Like a dark ceiling: down rushed the rain
> Impetuous; and continued till the earth
> No more was seen."—MILTON.

NOAH was directed to build an ark, the length of which was one hundred and sixty yards, breadth of beam twenty-seven yards, and sixteen yards high, and was in our parlance a three-decker, in which was to be collected male and female of all animated creation, together with Noah and his family, and food sufficient to supply this living cargo for the space of twelve months and ten days. An enlightened conscience admits that the flood came, and that the great end was accomplished, in accordance with God's holy purpose: which was the destruction of all of Adam's posterity who were not the immediate members of Noah's family: including those who had allied themselves to

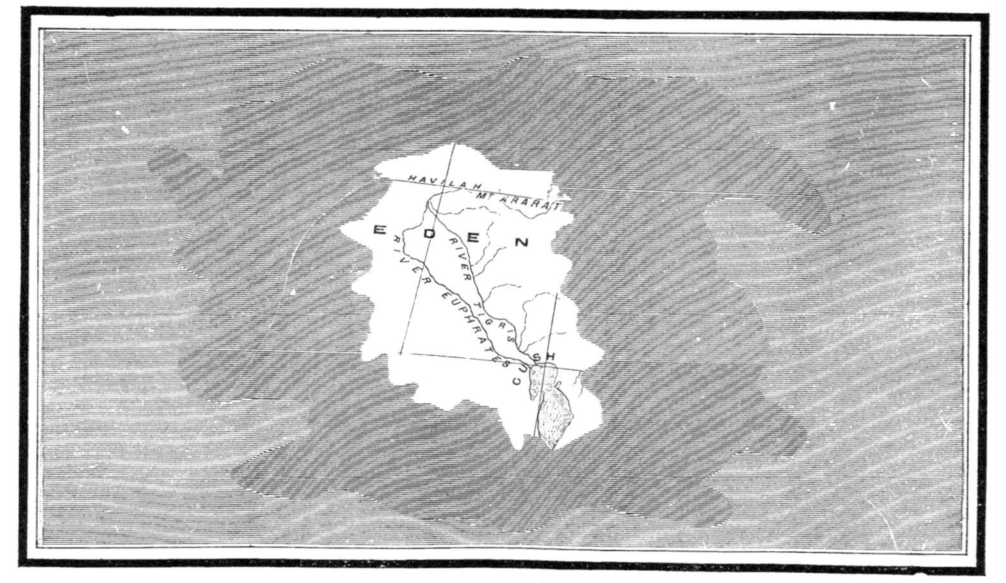

THE KNOWN WORLD AT THE DELUGE.

the aborigines of the East. All that portion of the world was deluged which at the time was known to the Adamite.

It is not our province to assume that any of the divine writers were or were not inspired as respects geography, astronomy, or geology, or, in fact, as respects any of the physical sciences; but this we know, that they addressed themselves to the understanding of their hearers, and in language appropriate to the knowledge of those who were to be enlightened. In the same style as the Roman would discourse in the days of the Cæsars, when speaking of the whole world; we understand him to include that portion of Asia, Europe, and Africa touching upon the Mediterranean Sea, and extending as far north as the isle of Britain.

In the same ratio do we reasonably conclude that the knowledge of the Israelites extended over but a very limited extent of the earth's surface. And thus to their understanding does Moses speak, when he transmits to his brethren the history of the Creation and the Deluge. Then only so much of the earth's surface was inundated as would accomplish the designs of Heaven, in visiting summary vengeance upon those of the chosen race who had wandered far from God and fallen from their high estate.

Noah was in the ark over twelve months, and six months had elapsed before the waters commenced to abate. And yet we find that Noah, at a still later period, sent forth a dove, which returned with an olive-leaf. The question here arises, whether or not the vegetable kingdom, immersed in water for nearly a year, would preserve vitality and put forth its leaf again.

I would sooner advance the more reasonable hypothesis that the dove had plucked the leaf from a higher elevation than the water had reached, or from sections less damaged by the overflow.

Josephus most certainly believed that the historian of the flood was inspired by Heaven, and I will here quote him:* "Now all the writers of the barbarian histories make mention of the flood and of this ark, among whom is Berossus the Chaldean. For when he was describing the circumstances of the flood he goes on thus: 'It is said there is some part of this ship in Armenia at the mountain of the Cordyæans; and that some people carry off pieces of the bitumen, which they take away and use chiefly as amulets for the averting of mischiefs.'

"Nay, Nicholas of Damascus, in his ninety-sixth book, hath a particular relation about them, where he speaks thus: 'There is a great mountain in Armenia, over Minyas, called Boris, upon which, it is reported, that many, who fled at the time of the deluge, were saved, and that one who was carried in an ark came on shore upon the top of it, and that the remains of the timber were a great while preserved. This might be the man about whom Moses, the legislator of the Jews, wrote.'"

We therefore must admit that the traditional record, even among the Jews, led them to believe that the entire surface was not covered, and that many who fled to the highest elevations escaped destruction. In reading ancient mythology, the tradition prevails also, in

* Antiquity of the Jews, chapter iii.

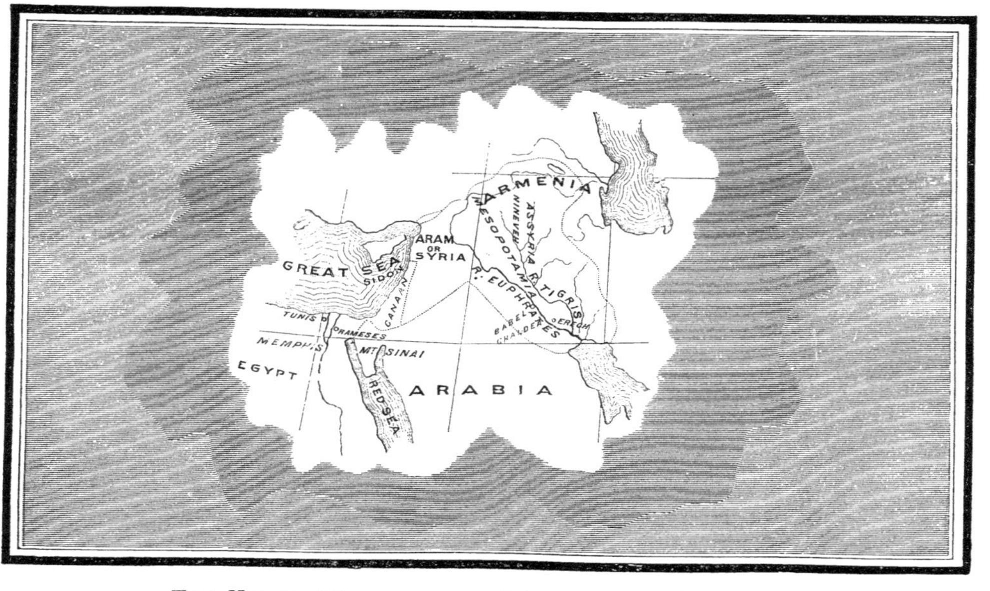

THE KNOWN WORLD AT THE EXODUS OF THE ISRAELITES.

Deucalion's flood, that many were preserved by ascending the highest mountains. If all animal life perished in the general flood save those which were turned loose on Ararat, why is it that we find on the continent of America at least twenty-five to thirty animals and birds entirely distinct from all other species yet discovered in the East and known to naturalists? The nearest point of America to Asia is eighteen miles, with a turbulent strait intervening; and many of these distinct races of animals found in America are known to avoid ordinary water-courses, much less launching out on the ocean for new discoveries. And if the suggestion is advanced that they crossed on the ice when the two shores were connected by the frozen element, then we urge the argument that the coldness, frigidity, and barrenness of that northern latitude must necessarily have proved fatal to those animals found in our more tropical clime, as observation and experience teaches us that the white polar bear cannot live even a day in a temperate zone without artificial cold.

By what process of reasoning, or by what magic thought, can we transport the indolent sloth of Patagonia from the resting-place of the ark to the southern extremity of South America?—an animal by no means given to locomotion, and at its usual rate of travel of nine feet per hour, would have required ten thousand years to have made such a hideous journey.* A journey,

---

* A striking illustration we find in the kangaroo and other animals that are alone found in Australia, fit companions too for the savages of that country. How did these animals get there? and how did the Malay find a home in this wilderness? I would suggest, however,

in fact, which that noble animal, the horse,* has never yet performed, though four thousand years have elapsed since the cargo of the ark was discharged on the mountains of Armenia.

Any person at all acquainted with the youthful science of geology may reasonably conclude that almost the entire face of the earth has at one period or other been submerged beneath the ocean, and by the convulsions of nature has been thrown up at various periods; and as the water retired to their ocean caverns, vegetation sprang up, and in the course of revolving ages life and animation peopled this once barren wilderness. It has been asserted that the upheaval of the American continent and the islands of the West had hurled upon the antediluvians that awful calamity which Noah's ark so bravely weathered. By no process of reasoning can such a flimsy theory be established, as every indication of nature goes to show the absurdity of such a position. The disintegration and preparation necessary for the surface to become a fit abode for plants, and the time necessarily required to elapse for the different particles to solidify and form masses of stone, where especially are imbedded the fossil débris of the animal and vegetable kingdoms, both of which have become extinct at periods where the memory of man runneth not to the

---

to the lover of the fabulous the legend of Europa, the daughter of the king of Phœnicia.

* The horse was not known in America until introduced here by the Spaniards, and yet "it is certain that the horse inhabited this country during the postpliocene period, long prior to the day when the present American Indian made his abode on this continent, as its fossil remains are found contemporaneously with the mastodon and megalonyx."

contrary. And again, there are living evidences in the vegetable kingdom of massive trees* whose record unmistakably indicates an age of at least five thousand to six thousand years. Even here where I write, this is, geologically speaking, a new country, and of very recent formation; yet we find deposits imbedded in the earth sixty and one hundred feet deep. The accretions thereupon accumulated were old when Adam first sang his lullaby to the goddess of morn, and plucked his first meal from the indigenous growth that adorned his earthly Paradise. Lest the reader may still be inclined to believe that the waters covered the entire hills and mountains of the globe, I will quote a few passages from the Bible in illustration of Biblical hyperbole, with no desire, however, to detract from the force of inspired truth, for on this basis alone I build my hopes for heaven and eternal life. Acts xxiv. 5: "We have found this man (Paul) a pestilent fellow, and a mover of sedition among *all the Jews throughout the world.*" No theologian is ready to declare that Paul had visited all the nations then occupied by the Jews. And Acts ii. 5: "There were dwelling at Jerusalem Jews, devout men, out of every nation under heaven." And again, Luke ii. 1: "And it came to pass in those days, that there went out a decree from Cæsar Augustus, *that all the world should be taxed.*" These passages are only presented to illustrate the position taken, that the world to the inspired historian comprised that portion that was known to man commercially, and thus he addressed himself to the understanding of his hearers. Should

* Trees declare their age by concentric circles.

the reader still be indisposed to admit our premises that the earth was partially covered with water, then I propose to establish my position by quoting one verse alone from the Bible, and prove to mankind that these inferior races of men did not all perish in the flood, but triumphantly made the voyage across the waste of waters, and, like the other creatures in that noble vessel, placed their feet on terra firma, and went forth beyond the Jordan of waters to fulfill their destinies, shaped as each was by the hand of a kind Providence. I know that you feel some interest to read that verse in the Scriptures of divine truth which did admit into the ark all the pre-adamic creatures.* Gen. vii. 15: "And they went in unto Noah into the ark, two and two of all flesh, wherein is the breath of life."

* "We are left free to accept the plain proofs furnished by astronomy and mechanics, by geology and physical geography, that the Deluge could not have been universal, unless the laws of all nature had been suspended."—PHILIP SMITH.

CHAPTER VI.

MAN AND THE QUADRUMANA TRIBES COMPARED.

"Ill-fated race: the softening arts of peace
Whate'er the harmonizing Muses teach:
The Godlike wisdom of the tempered breast,
Progressive truth, the patient force of thought:
Investigation calm—the government of laws,
These are not theirs."—THOMSON.

IN this chapter I shall discourse of the negro, together with the other inferior races, in contradistinction to man, or the Adamite.

In Bible language the Caucasian is man, the noblest work of God. The negro, with his cotemporary races, is the creature erroneously called the beast. I appeal to the Bible. Tell me, thou reverend chronicler of antiquity, can the vain sophistry of the learned overturn or controvert the established fulfillments of divine revelation?

Gen. i. 24 and 25: "And God said, Let the earth bring forth the *living creature* after his kind, cattle, and creeping thing, and *beast* of the earth after his kind: and it was so. And God made the *beast* of the earth after his kind, and cattle after their kind, and every thing that creepeth upon the earth after his kind." And again, Gen. iii. 1: "Now the *serpent was more subtil than any beast of the field* which the Lord God had made." Showing conclusively the superiority of the *creature* over the *beast* of the field, for the *creature* in his craftiness had beguiled the woman, and the Lord cursed him thus: "Thou art cursed above all cattle, and above every beast of the field; upon thy belly shalt thou go, and dust shalt thou eat all the days of thy life;" that is, thou shalt be the lowest class in the scale of being, abject, debased, and deceitful, mean, contemptible, and despicable in the eyes of my chosen people, whom thou, by the wily craftiness of your tutelar deity, Lucifer, you have essayed to bring to the level of your own infamy and degradation.

Creature thou art, but not a man in the image and likeness of your Creator. Groveling in nature, and possessing none of the higher traits of nobility that bespeak an assimilation to the ennobling attributes derived from Deity, and which impresses upon the soul the unmistakable stamp of a higher and more exalted origin. God was once manifested to us in the flesh. Did He come in the form and likeness of either one of the inferior races? He presented Himself to us in the image of his Father, clothed upon with all the paraphernalia that indicated a direct descent from Adam. Christ was the God-man, a true Caucasian of the blushing race, the highest type of the original creation; endowed with beauty of person, symmetry of form and feature, and devoid of that organism expressive of brutal force and destructiveness, and of sensuality and its accompanying elements of baseness; his brow beaming with intelligence and his heart melting with compassion. The dignity of his mien, the expressive character of his organization, the noble combination of worth and intellectuality that are exhibited in his structure and exemplified in his daily intercourse with man, stamp him in the highest degree the noblest and the best of earthly cotemporaries.

Reverting to the mistranslation of *creature*, I will quote from Revelation iv. 6–8: "And before the throne there was a sea of glass like unto crystal: and in the midst of the throne, and round about the throne, were four *beasts* full of eyes before and behind. And the first *beast* was like a lion, and the second *beast* like a calf, and the third *beast* had a face as a man, and the fourth *beast* was like a flying eagle. And the four *beasts* had each of them six wings about him; and they were full of eyes within: and they rest not day and night, saying, Holy, holy, holy, Lord God Almighty, which was, and is, and is to come." The first impulse of enlightened nature would tell us that there were no beasts in heaven. These were creatures paying adoration around the throne of God, and constituted a part of the heavenly host. We read in Jer. xxi. 6: "And I will smite the inhabitants of this city, both *man and beast:* they shall die of a great pestilence." And again, in Jonah iii. 7 and 8: "And he caused it to be proclaimed and published through Nineveh by the decree of the king and his nobles, saying, Let neither man nor *beast,* herd nor flock, taste any thing: let them not feed, nor drink water: but let *man and beast be covered with sackcloth, and cry mightily unto God:* yea, let them turn every one from his evil way, and from the violence that is in their hands."

Were these real beasts who are threatened above with summary vengeance, and required to put on sackcloth and cry mightily unto God? or were they captives from the land of Confucius, or slaves from the islands of Polynesia or the gold coast of Africa?

Nearly all modern zoologists contend that the various races of mankind are included under one genus, man, and are characterized by possessing two hands, and are distinguished from the monkey or ape tribes on the ground that the ape is supplied with four hands. We herein observe the distinctive features existing between the bimana and the quadrumana races of the mammalia family.

Dr. Darwin, however, seems to class us all originally as quadrumana, and by successive improvements upon the original stock the Caucasian, it seems, has leaped, like the goddess Minerva, pure, perfect, and undefiled from the troubled brain of some giant of the chimpanzee or gorilla tribes. This theory reversed, in the course of a few centuries, would carry the doctor and his followers back to the quadrumana, and it might prove a mortification to their pride to find the caudal appendage assuming its wonted position at the lower terminus of the vertebra. From considerations, however, of nobler aspirations, I should demur to this theory, and endeavor to found the temple of human greatness on a foundation more refined and sublimated than the skull of the ourang-outang, and with unfeigned disgust I should look back upon my humble progenitor and exclaim, "Worthy son of a degenerate sire!"

The gorilla belongs to the genus troglodytes, and is regarded as the highest of the anthropoid apes. He is exceedingly ferocious when found in his native wilds, on the west coast of Africa, both above and below the equator. The adult male grows to the height of five or six feet, and is strong and muscular, and when aroused is regarded as a more formidable enemy than the lion or tiger. The limbs are well developed and of great strength. Their arms are longer than those of the chimpanzee, extending far down the leg, but not to the ankle, as with the ourang-outang. The skull of the male is longer and wider, but less heavy, than that of man, and the capacity of the cavity which contains the brain is less than one-half of that of the most degraded human races.* The gorilla bears a nearer resemblance to the human type than any other of the ape species, and this resemblance is more manifest and striking in the young of those two races than in the adults; and as each matures in form this striking resemblance diminishes, and widens the disparity between the two.†

Whatever of appearance, either in structure, form, habit, or likeness, that may indicate a common origin to all the races, even including that of the quadrumana, is exploded at a glance by the observations of the practical anatomist. So far as the ourang-outang is concerned, a ten-year-old boy would revolt at the idea of recognizing him as a brother,—with his hands reaching to his ankles, or with the chimpanzee, reaching below the knees, with short lower extremities, flat and retiring forehead, and with peculiar physical frame, that

---

* The author of the Arabian tales reminds us of the similarity existing between man and his prototype, when he describes the conflict between the *old man of the sea* and one of his less fortunate adventurers.

† New American Cyclopædia.

allies the whole tribe more intimately with the quadruped tribes than with either of the lower types of the genus homo. The ourang-outang and chimpanzee are always found in a very hot climate: the former under the equator, in the Indian Archipelago, and the latter in Africa only, and principally on the Congo and Guinea coasts; and neither can survive for any length of time even in a temperate zone.

The most striking difference found to exist among the various types of the human family is observed in the facial angle of the skull; and by measurement it is established that the facial angle of the Caucasian is larger than the corresponding angle in either of the lower tribes of our species, which illustrates the never-to-be-forgotten fact that larger space for brain is allotted to the Adamic race, for purposes of intellectuality and the practice of virtue, and less for the brutal passions and native instincts of our nature, than is developed even in the highest type of the Mongolian. And in the peculiar formation of the skull of the inferior tribes of Africa, the least space is allotted for the development of brain, for the exhibition of intellect, the basis of moral worth, goodness, and excellence. On the Gold Coast of Africa, and with the aborigines of Australia, we find a class of savages which should scarcely be denominated human beings: they are but a shade more elevated than the very brute that inhabits this planet, and cannot be distinguished as human either by habit, custom, dress, or form of religion, and we can only discern the shadow of the man in his erect form and linguistic peculiarities.

Remember that man is the only animal that can

stand on his feet in a natural position, or is able for any length of time to walk erect.

Looking closely at the characteristic traits of these barbarous hordes, can the intelligent mind behold any lineament in their feature, form, or nature that would induce us to hail them as lineal descendants of Adam, of Noah, or of Abraham: with a head prognathous in character, depressed in front, and wanting in elevation of forehead; their cheek-bones projecting forward, their jaws lengthened, and the entire face elongated; with teeth projecting to the front as though nature intended that they should arrest their food and supply their appetites like the carnivorous animals of the forest? They have brain, it is true; so has the hog, the ass, and the jackal. Where is the cranial capacity to contain the elements of sense, intellectuality, and progress, which the retreating form of the forehead disallows? The nostrils are wide and extended like a war-horse on the rampage, and the nose itself is destitute of that small nasal bone, or cartilage, which supports and gives prominence to that feature, and adds lustre to the countenance of the Caucasian. The apertures are large and the olfactories well developed; the lip is thick and heavy, indicative of sensuality in the extreme; in fact, this vice crops out at every pore of his beastly nature.

Zoologists say that there is a marked difference not only in the thicker skull of the negro and the smallness of the facial angle, but also in the formation of the pelvis; and it requires no great skill on the part of the scientific anatomist to detect, by the marks of the denuded skeleton, the proper race to which each subject belongs.

The type of the negro as to cranium is prognathous; the Mongolian pyramidal; and the Caucasian elliptical. And by measurement it has been fixed, on an average, that the facial angle in the ourang-outang extends from 30° to 35°; in the negro the angle extended is 70°; in the Asiatic, 75°; and in the Caucasian, 80°. Showing most conclusively, as advanced in the beginning of these pages, that the material creation was not only gradual and progressive, but that the animal creation were also in the same order and progression in their physical formations and intellectual tendencies, all of which was an essential part of nature's programme, and constituted an established purpose in the divine economy.

In speaking of the physical distinctions prominent in the two races, the sole of the white man's foot is concave, and the weight of the body rests upon an arch; and wherever you find his track impressed upon the sands of time, you immediately recognize it from the foot-print of the Congo and Guinea inhabitant, the hollow of whose foot, in common parlance, makes a hole in the ground. The vertebra, or spinal column, in the negro has its idiosyncrasy, which the eye of the common observer readily detects, and stamps on his frame apparent deformity, which ever fits him for and renders him a suitable subject as the bearer of burdens, and ennobles him in his sphere as a hewer of wood and a drawer of water for a wiser and a more enterprising race.

The color* of the skin is a matter of importance

* "WHY THE NEGRO WAS CREATED BLACK.—That the negro was formed for the climate of Africa the whole structure of his body

which should by no means be left out of consideration, and is said to exist alone in the epidermis, or outer covering of the body; and at the base of this cuticle is secreted that odoriferous musk which so eminently distinguishes this race from all others that ever came from the plastic hand of the Creator.

An idea prevails with some that unwholesome food and the filthy habits of the negro engender this peculiar odor that is so obnoxious to the more sensitive olfactories of the intelligent and refined. To satisfy the incredulous the experiment has been tried, where similar diet, ablution, and sanitary measures have been equally and impartially administered to the subjects of both races, and on coming out of the fiery ordeal of purification, it is still manifest that the germ is there, and that the aroma of the Ethiopian is still volatile and uncompromising in its nature. Tell me, ye guardian angel that hovers over my destiny and points back

---

unites to prove. First, as a protection to the brain against the direct rays of the sun, his hair is made to grow short and curly, and he is furnished with a skull of enormous thickness. In no other being do we see the wisdom of the Creator more clearly exhibited than in the construction of the African. The soles of his feet are overlaid with a thick layer of fat,—a bad conductor of heat,—thereby enabling him to walk at ease over the burning sands, and forming for him a far better protection than any contrivance the art of man could devise. And now you may ask, Why did God make the African black? I answer, In order that he may be able to keep cool in that torrid climate. A black surface will radiate or part with heat much more rapidly than a white one, an experiment that any one may try. Take two vessels that are in every respect the same,—two teapots, for instance; let one of them be covered over with lamp-black, then fill both with boiling water, and you will find the black one will be cold much sooner than the bright one."

through a long line of ancestral ages, can the leopard change his spots, or the Ethiopian change his skin? I once was young and buoyant in spirit as the morning lark or sportive lamb; and in days of childhood, as the innocent prattler would dangle upon his mother's knee, and learned to lisp her name in love, and hearken to the sweet accents that fell from her cherished lips, and her heart full of the intuitive emotions that burst from a Christian soul; and later still in life, when music charms the unhallowed ear, and the troubled heart vibrates in consonance with the deep-toned sigh that escapes from lovely beauty, at whose feet I sit and dream my life away, tell me, ye beau ideal of primeval hope and yet untasted joys, does the unrefined blood of the sable Ethiopian course through those purple veins which mine eye traces along that arm of snowy white? And does it suffuse that tender cheek with crimson hues when the heart overflows with reciprocated affection? Are those gentle eyes, or golden locks, or raven curls fed by the same crimson fluid which gives life to the olive tribes of Central Asia or the dark-visaged sons of North and South America? Tell me, ye loved ones, in truth and sincerity, are we allied by blood and consanguinity to the dark aboriginal races, whose form, color, custom, and religion are repulsive to our senses, and whose laws, habits, and religious rites are universally opposed to divine revelation and inimical to the progress and advancement of our species? Tell me, once more, my guardian angel, can the leopard change his spots, or the Ethiopian change his skin?

This question was propounded nearly three thousand years ago to the descendants of Abraham by the prophet

Jeremiah, xiii. 23: "Can the Ethiopian change his skin, or the leopard his spots? then may ye also do good, that are accustomed to do evil." The theory is advanced by all who advocate the unity of the races, that the variety of color, hair, and anatomical structure, apparent among the different races of the human species, is solely attributable to the change of climate, food, habits, and manners of the various tribes who are occupying the different continents of the globe. The advocates of this theory, then, give the lie to the declaration of the prophet Jeremiah when he asked the above question. The answer is implied that neither the Asiatic, African, nor the leopard could change his color, unless man can change his own nature and regenerate his own soul: if this be feasible, then Christ hath died in vain.

The tropical sun may burn the skin and mar the beauty of the blushing race. But can it destroy his color, and change his physical organization, and produce such a hideous revolution that a mother could not recognize her first-born child? Verily not, though they should survive from the moment when the sun of day first illumined the bespangled sky to the hour when "eternal hope shall light her torch at nature's funeral pile."

Examine under a microscope the hair of a white man and the wool of a negro, and the tale is soon told that there is a cavity, or hollow, as observed in the oat or rye straw, throughout the entire length of the one, whereas the genuine black African's crispy wool in appearance and texture is solid throughout, and more closely allied to the wool that grows on the back of certain quadrupeds,—rather a plausible argument in favor of the Darwinian theory. Again, the black skin of this race does not burn or blister even under a tropical sun. I have seen the black man of Louisiana throw off his shirt in our broiling summer's sun and with impunity labor for hours and days as a matter of choice, and the direct rays would have no more effect upon his back than a mosquito's proboscis on the impenetrable hide of an alligator; while the true Saxon under an hour's exposure would cringe like a beast under his burden, and would peel off like a snake when making his *début* on the return of spring.

The dark races, on principles of sound philosophy, were created to occupy the belt of the torrid and temperate zones, and wherever, by the fate of circumstance or the *vi et armis* of their warlike neighbors, they have violated this established principle of their nature and located in high northern latitudes, they become dwarfish in stature, and lose whatever of energy they may have formerly possessed, become less prolific and more assimilated to the indigenous surroundings of that elevated and frozen region, as is thoroughly exemplified in the case of the Esquimaux and the inhabitants of Lapland, of whom, with the Finns and other kindred tribes of Siberia, I shall speak in due course of time. And, as regards the negro, the experienced observer readily knows that a very cold climate freezes him out, and that nowhere under the expanded canopy of heaven does he flourish to the same extent as he does within his native geographical sphere; and, as has been asserted by his defenders, that in every instance where he has been removed to a colder or more elevated region, he becomes bleached and whitened by coming in contact with a fairer race of people.

Truly, we see that exemplified in our own America, where the African assumes a Caucasian physiognomy, which can be explained readily on the most rational grounds imaginable. Amalgamation comes to his relief, and the negro whitens in shades of color, and his hair straightens also, and changes in texture in the same proportion as you infuse into his veins more of the Turanian or Saxon blood. A cross among the domestic animals of a truly high-blooded character with one of a lower grade must enhance the worth of the inferior, and diminish the value of the superior in the same ratio.

CHAPTER VII.

THE MALAY.

> "The ocean spreads
> O'er coral rocks and amber beds,
> Where sandal-groves and bowers of spice
> Might be a Peri's Paradise,
> But human blood—the smell of Death—
> Mingles its taint with every breath."—MOORE.

ZOOLOGICALLY and geographically speaking, the human family have been divided, by common consent, into five different races, from which hypothesis I am not seriously disposed to appeal, and will therefore treat the subject with a view to the distinctions already made.

5*

Pickering, however, advances the supposition that there are at least eleven distinct races of the human genus now extant, while Desmoulins asserts that there are fully sixteen; and Agassiz and Nott contend that there are an indefinite number of species, who were created originally in groups, some of whom are no doubt extinct, while others still occupy the land of their forefathers.

By the arrangement as first intimated, the next race in order after the African proper is the Malay, the next highest type. But before proceeding farther let me call your attention to the admitted fact that there are found more noticeable varieties and shades among the negro tribes than are comprised even among our own race, estimating from the lowest grade to the most exalted character.

The Malay tribes, generally speaking, occupy Malacca, Madagascar, and Oceanica. In fact, we may include the East Indian and Polynesian Archipelagoes; and, by the way, this division of mankind is more widely distributed on the globe possibly than any other race of whom it is our purpose to discourse, and their habits, manners, and social condition exhibit greater variety than all the other inferior races combined. The population of this area occupied by the Malay is computed at one hundred and twenty millions of souls.

The complexion of this race is a reddish brown, assuming the hue of burnished copper, and is not altogether uniform, but is darker than the Mongolian, but lighter than many of the mixed tribes of the African coast. The hair is very straight, coarse, and black as jet, and hangs profusely abundant on the scalp. The beard naturally is very thin, and the custom prevails with them almost universally to pluck it out. The lips are thick and the nose flattened; the latter at maturity sometimes assumes an aquiline appearance. The head is retreating, with small facial angle, with brain-cavity larger than the negro, but far less than the Indo-European. Their features and complexion are modified more or less in different latitudes, as well as they present to us greater advancement or debasement in accordance with the adulteration of blood, whether obtained from a higher or lower type of the human family, which explains readily the distinction drawn by historians of their civilization or their barbarism.

They have a characteristic fondness for roving, which accounts for their distribution throughout the various islands of the sea, ranging from the coast of Africa east to the islands on the west of North America. They are a cowardly people, cunning, treacherous, and vindictive, and will nurse their smothered resentment and diabolic designs under every manifestation of good will and affection until the desired opportunity presents itself, and then pounce upon their victim like a wolf upon the fold.

They have, by way of misnomer, been called civilized in part, but verily they are all barbarous; emphatically so, I imagine, as the incident is fresh now in the memory of not a few living that they devoured the first missionaries who ventured among them to convert them to the true religion, as also did the natives of the Sandwich Islands slay and eat the memorable Captain Cook while on one of his voyages circumnavigating the globe; while to this day they are universally noted for their piratical proclivities, ignorance, and baseness of character; and, as before remarked, that destiny has fixed their habitation under the equatorial line, where their appetites are fed by the native fruits that ripen in every season, and where the labor of other nations fall into their hands, and is appropriated by that spirit of rapine and plunder which they have honestly inherited from their aboriginal progenitors. This race, though isolated in part, and separated from each other thousands of miles by oceans of water intervening, and severing entirely even the probability of any social or commercial intercourse having existed among them for the space of thousands of years; and yet, amidst this seclusion and fixed isolation, we trace an undeniable singularity and sameness of language, feature, manners, habits, and configuration of person, which fixes an identity that defies contradiction, and must bring stern conviction to the mind of every unbiased thinker.

As with all other distinct races, however, there are minor differences apparent in color, form, and general outline, which is superinduced by mixing with other races, either more enlightened or more savage than they, or possessing other shades of color derived from an intercourse with surrounding nations.* Yet their distinctness and identity of race cannot be mistaken,

---

* The Malay is so much adulterated with the Mongolian in some localities, and with the African in other places, that some ethnologists are disposed to regard them as distinct species; and truly there is an improvement for the better where the infusion is derived from the former, while an admixture of the latter only tends to deteriorate and debase the standard.

though always found anatomically allied to the lower or prognathous type as respects cranial formation.

With regard to the intellectual and monumental developments displayed by the Malayan, together with the other four races inhabiting this planet, I shall speak of them more particularly at another place.

CHAPTER VIII.

THE AMERICAN INDIAN.

In rolling flood, in wind and storm,
Where mountain crag and hoary steep
Arise and spread each airy form
Amid ethereal skies that weep—
Here history can no tale unfold,
Here sprang to life from Nature's mould
The Indian chief, the warrior bold.

THE next race in order which engrosses our attention is the American Indian, whom Columbus and cotemporary discoverers found occupying almost the entire continent of America. It has already been intimated that the Esquimaux of the north more properly belonged originally to the Turanian race, and we will likewise include in the same category certain tribes of Mexico, Central America, and Peru, leaving a very large majority of the aborigines of this country as belonging to the third ethnological division of the human family.

The peculiarities of this race are high cheek-bones, protruding jaws, eyes deep-seated, nose broad but prominent, lips full and rounded, skin brown or cinnamon colored, beard scanty, hair black, long, and straight, with features distinctly marked and prominent. The shape of the head is square, with low forehead, and form of skull entirely different from the types before described, and differing materially from the Central Asiatic.

Dr. Prichard, who has spent a long life in the advocacy of the unity of the human family, thus discourses, "that all the different races aboriginal in the American continent belong, as far as their history and language have been investigated, to one family of nations, and that these races display considerable diversities in their physical constitution, though derived from one stock, and still betraying indications of mutual resemblance, and that, as existing two centuries ago, that they did not present any certain evidence of derivation from any special old world race."

The features of the Indian are frequently regular and the expression noble, and in many instances the females are regarded as handsome. Their muscular frame in many respects does not compare with that of the white man, but his powers of endurance in the wild hunt for game or for the scalp of his enemy, subsisting for days upon a mere pittance, is far above that of our own race under similar circumstances of exposure. The complexion varies in different latitudes, owing to various causes, and the physical stature also is not uniform, the average height varying in certain localities from ten to twelve inches. But one feature peculiar to the native

American should not be lost sight of; that those tribes found nearest to the poles have not been whitened by the frosts and snows of a colder latitude, while the Toltican or Mexico-Peruvian tribes are not only fairer than their more distant neighbors, but decidedly more intelligent and progressive in their tendencies. The facial angle is only 75°, and the volume of the brain is only 79 cubic inches for the semi-civilized, and 84 for the more barbarous tribes, while the low, retreating forehead diminishes space for the development of the intellectual faculties, whereas the posterior lobes of the brain are much larger with the inferior races, showing a preponderance on the side of brute force and native depravity. The Indian naturally is haughty and reserved in his bearing to strangers, and stoical and uncompromising in his character. He recognizes no neutral ground, and ignores frankly every condition of life that prompts the emotions of humanity. When war becomes the order of the day, he flaunts to the breeze the black flag of extermination, asks no quarter and gives none in return. By his creed the captive belongs to the victor, and mercy pleads in vain for its victim. Age and sex are without an advocate when the war-whoop of the savage resounds through the land. In peace he is indolent and grave, and when the stranger approaches his wigwam he is received with kindness, and the hospitalities of his board are offered without stint. He is grateful to a friend, never forgets a kindness, and never forgives a foe. The peculiar cranial formation is such with all of the inferior races of man, that the intellectual is so far overshadowed by the animal propensities that his elevation in the scale of being is almost a matter of impossibility. The Indian, more than any other race under the sun, is devoted to warfare, and differs from John Chinaman, who wears his queue behind; the native American boasts a scalp-lock on the top of his head, and defies the world in arms, and rash is he who essays to snatch this trophy in the hour of conflict. The encroachments made by their superiors upon this unfortunate people have reduced their numbers to about fifteen million souls. The treachery and savage disposition of his nature, it is to be presumed, is not altogether unknown to the Anglo-American, though the latter has done much to provoke his wrath and bring upon him the fires of extermination.

It seems strange, on reflection, that the enlightened world is so ready and willing to strike hands with and call the Indian and the negro "hail brother, well met," of one blood and of one bone, and offspring of one and the same pair of parents. Child of light, son of civilization, worshiper of the first-born, why, in Heaven's name, has the white man treated his brother thus? With flame and sword ye came and spoiled his land, ye entered his wigwam and partook of his hospitable meal, and warmed your limbs at the blazing fire that burned on his humble hearth; and in the dead hour of the stilly night, when gentle slumbers and placid dreams inwrapped the prostrate forms of the helpless sleepers, you bathed your knife in the hearts of your unsuspecting victims. With the power of might you robbed him of his possessions, and drove him a wanderer from the home of his forefathers, and converted his fair domain into a desert, which proved more repulsive to his feelings than the great Sahara to the nomadic hordes of the East. And when he came and told his tale of sorrow, and pointed to the mound where stood the unpretending hut of his warrior chief, and marked on the ground with his palsied finger where reposed the consecrated ashes of his people for a thousand generations, and demanded a consideration for the hunting-grounds of his fathers, you laughed at his calamity, and mocked at the gushing sorrow of his soul, and said, "Thou dotard, flee to your forest chambers and your mountain home, and await thou patiently until the desolating besom shall sweep the last vestige of your race from the continent of America. This alone shall be your consideration. Might is right, and before that altar we bow, worship, and adore." Has the black man no tale of sorrow to relate? no cause to reproach his pale-faced brother? snatched from his native country unapprised, the untold horrors of the middle passage, sold in a foreign land, and doomed to slavery for ages to come! I repeat, it is strange that the truly enlightened heart should entertain convictions of the unity of the human family and treat his dark-visaged brother with such unbecoming brutality; whereas views of a plurality of the races would in the eyes of many modify the guilt to some extent, but not justify such a course of conduct by any means.

There can be no doubt, however, of the distinctness and unity of this race of people. Their language is exclusively original with themselves, and is not found to correspond in root or branch with any of the known languages whom the researches of the Indo-European has yet had the good fortune to analyze; and their peculiar religious views and manners and habits of life are so at variance with all other nations under the sun, that our most scientific and observant judges of the human species assign to them an originality and diversity of traits of character and physical formation which must place them distinct and aboriginal in the general creation of the world, and as the Aryan would say, they are the autochthones of the land.

It is impossible at this late day, without written records or direct revelation, to fix beyond the possibility of a doubt in the minds of all any maxim, however nearly it may approach the truth of an established axiom in mathematics; we will always find some theorist whose ideas are antagonistic, and whose views run off invariably at a tangent. This position is illustrated in the varied religions of the day, where each sect claims exact harmony with divine revelation itself; whereas their interpretations of holy writ are as much at variance as the antipodes.

CHAPTER IX.

THE MONGOLIAN.

The work of man, is man to study well
Where'er he move, or where the races dwell,
On barren shores, or in the tropic belt,
Or where alternate heat and cold are felt,—
Mongolia sits on Asia's arid plain,
Nor calls us man beyond her wide domain.

THE next race in order for our consideration is the ancient Central Asiatic or Mongolian race, whom Professor Max Müller has, in these latter days, denominated the Turanian, in consideration of the contest waged between the Aryan family and Turan, the representative of the great Tartar family, and only second in importance to the linguist and ethnologist after the Indo-European and Semitic tribes, who are the lineal descendants of Noah. This type of mankind originally dwelt east of Eden, occupying Central and Northern Asia, and ultimately spreading over the most, if not entire Europe, the polar belt of North America, and other districts of the American and Asiätic continents. Though an inferior race, compared with the Caucasian, in point of intellectual capacity, its migrations and occupancy abroad have been more extended than any other single race of the genus homo, and has performed a more important part in the political history of the world. There is a marked similarity in the language of this race, though scattered over such a vast territory, and subject, too, to innovations from all sides. It is formed on what is termed the agglutinative type: the root under no circumstances undergoes any change, and in giving expression to the ideas formed in the mind syllables are suffixed, and form no close and intimate union, but remain in the condition of loosely appended words,—a marked peculiarity known to no other language or people under the canopy of heaven.

The Mongolian's manners, customs, habits of life, and cranial formation differ materially from all other races with whom we are acquainted, and belong to that division of the species usually denominated pyramidal form of skull; they are stout, swarthy, and ugly, possessing a broad, flat face and prominent cheek-bones, high and broad shoulders, thick, short necks, and bony and nervous hands. Their eyes are black and drawn at the corners, which gives them an elliptical appearance. Their noses are considerably flattened, and their complexion varies slightly from a yellow or olive hue to a more swarthy color. The hair is universally straight, dark, coarse, and is worn usually in a queue behind. This race is not so tall in stature as the Caucasian or the American Indian, and differs so materially from these two races that it requires no experienced eye to locate the Mongolian, wherever found, when pure in blood and uncontaminated by alliance with other races. They inhabited Central Asia originally, but now occupy Northern, Central, and Eastern Asia, and as far south as the limits of the Malayan territory. As remarked previously, the Finns and Lapps of the north of Europe and the Esquimaux of North America justly belong to this race, and there are many reasons why we should also include in the same family those nations whom the Spaniards conquered at an early day, under the leadership of Pizarro and Cortes,—the aboriginal occupants of Peru, Central America, and Mexico.

The Mongolian is marked with every shade of color, just in proportion as his blood has been tinged with that of other nations of a lighter or darker hue. The original department of the eastern hemisphere formerly allotted to the Adamic race, that is, Western Asia, has in times past been overrun by the Central Asiatic, and one time they in fact overran and occupied almost the entire continent of Europe, and that portion of Africa embraced between the Great Desert and the Mediterranean Sea. These Oriental hordes, warlike and barbarous in their habits, had become cramped in their ancient allotted territory, oppressed by laws every way tyrannical in their enforcement, trampled upon and enslaved by the satraps of that densely-populated region, came out from thence in swarms like the devouring locusts, and spread themselves over Western Asia and the continent of Europe; and for the time being, the dominant race of the world, in point of intellect and progress, had to succumb to the triumphant hordes of the aggressive Mongolian. Had these warlike successes continued on the part of this inferior race, and they had remained in the ascendant, with all the nations of earth subdued to their will, our condition, intellectually, morally, and religiously, would have been deplorable indeed. But, fortunately for the cause of civilization and humanity, the Caucasian rose phœnix-like, by the might of his transcendent genius, and drove out the Mongol tribes, and confined them on the south to the fastness of the Pyrenees Mountains, and on the north to the icy coast of Scandinavia, where the Finn and the Lapp to-day ekes out a mere existence in a latitude too frozen in its temperature to suit his dark-visaged nature. Much on a par are these restricted tribes with their fellow-wanderers in Alaska, Siberia, Kamschatka, and the inhabitants of the Aleutian Archipelago. In Hungary is found a remnant of this people under the style of the Magyars, who settled there about the fourth century after Christ.

And in Turkey we have the Ottoman, whose blood has been much purified, and whose pyramidal cast of cranium has been considerably modified by an admixture of the blood of the Circassian and Georgian girls, whom avarice and an entire want of parental affection have introduced as slaves in the Turkish market. Nor is this manifest appearance of change of feature and cranial formation confined to the noble and the wealthy alone, but extends to every class and grade of the Ottoman Empire, and is thoroughly understood when we call to mind that the white damsel of Caucasus is valued in the slave-markets of the East according to beauty and symmetry of feature and figure, and that the more homely commands a much less price, and thereby comes within the range of the poorer aspirant for connubial joys; and the entire want of virtue and chastity with these hybrid races, which has been proverbial from the earliest ages, would essentially change the Mongolian characteristics and approximate his standard to that of the Caucasian.

The same, to a certain extent, is observed in Persia, the land of Cyrus and Xerxes, which, in ages gone by, yielded to the conquering tramp of the Eastern hordes, and permitted its bright escutcheon to be tarnished with the olive tinge; while others of original Persian extraction have preserved intact the purity of the Semitic race, like the high-blooded Castilian and the proud sons of Aragon have alone, among the inhabitants of the Spanish peninsula, kept aloof from the degenerate blood introduced through successive ages in the south of Europe. The Spaniard, the Portuguese, and the Italian are everlasting monuments of hybrid degeneracy.

When man mocks at Deity and violates the fixed laws of his being, he must suffer loss, the iniquities of which are visited upon him to the third and fourth generation. Who remembers when the Roman standard was planted upon the isle of Britain, and the inhabitants of the known world, from the sands of Asia to the uttermost parts of the earth, brought their diadems and laid them suppliantly at the feet of the Cæsars, —when Spain sent forth her navies and planted the cross in the temple of the Incas and Mexican adorers of the sun, and the Toltecs of America became vassals, and emptied their treasures into the lap of the proud and exacting Spaniard. The Spanish and Portuguese conquests in America and elsewhere have passed from under their yoke, and these once flourishing nations, though still proud and arrogant in spirit, have lost all the noble genius of enterprise and progress once possessed, and have dwindled down to third- and fourth-rate powers among the nationalities of earth; and the hybrid races of this continent, founded by these dynasties, are everlasting monuments of that degeneracy resulting from the amalgamation of ours with an inferior race in the scale of being. Where the Mongol has crossed with other races of a lower type, we find in that type quite an improvement, physiologically and intellectually as well as in shade of color. For instance, there is a vast improvement in the Hottentots and Bushmen of Southern Africa, and the Ashantees, Dahomans, and Senegambians of Western Africa. Some of the latter, however, are slightly tinged with the Caucasian, from the intercourse that originally existed between the Mediterranean tribes and the western coast of Africa, while the Hindoo* has a slight infusion of the Adamic stock as well as a heavy supply of the Malay admixture. In fact, wherever intercourse, from whatever cause, arises between distinct races, it is as natural for them to mix as wine and water, which must ever account for the variety of shades and colors continually turning up in different localities, and not, as some authors have

* "It is a great mistake to suppose that all India is peopled by a single race, or that there is not as great a disparity between the inhabitants of Guzerat, Bengal, the Doab, and the Deccan, both in language, manners, and physiognomy, as between any four nations of Europe."—BISHOP HEBER.

"The general complexion of the people is dark brown, though many are as black as negroes, while the Parsees and people of Cashmere, in the north, are but little darker than the inhabitants of Southern Europe. . . . They have black and straight hair, and are usually well formed."—*American Cyclopædia.*

assigned, attributable to the influences of localities as respects heat and cold.

The Mongolian race comprises nearly one-half of the human family, and is estimated to number five hundred and sixty million souls, and is the only one of all the aboriginal races who has left, or now has in preservation, one solitary monument of architectural or intellectual ingenuity. The negro, Malay, and American Indian have nothing better than a thatched or mud dwelling; and the Indian has left the solitary relic of earthen mounds, scattered hither and thither, intended, no doubt, as a memorial of some victory achieved over a neighboring warlike race, or as a tomb to perpetuate the virtues of some brave chieftain of his tribe, by which they are justly denominated the mound-builders.

In consideration of this development of mechanical skill and intellectual advancement, as well as peculiar physiological formation and linguistic affinities, induces me to include the Aztec, the Toltec, and the Incas kindred races, as certainly a part and parcel of the great Central Asiatic families. The Toltecs dwelt on the north of the valley of Mexico prior to the arrival of the Aztecs, the latter of whom are claimed, by some writers, to be the founders of the ancient Mexican civilization. But really the Toltecs are the party to whom this distinguished honor is due. Their capital was Tula, and the remains of many magnificent build ings were still to be seen when the Spaniards first invaded Mexico, and the name Toltec has justly become synonymous with architect. Prescott says, "The Toltecs were well instructed in agriculture and many of the most useful mechanic arts; were nice workers of metal; invented the complex arrangement of time adopted by the Aztecs, and in short were the true fountains of the civilization which distinguished this part of the continent in latter times." The Incas were the chiefs or imperial heads of the great Peruvian Empire in the fifteenth century, and this chain of semi-civilization extended from the highlands north of the valley of Mexico, through Yucatan, Guatemala, and across the Andes to the broad alluvians of the Amazon and Orinoco. How they reached these latitudes and became a dominant race in the midst of these mound-builders may be explained on the theory that the immense population concentrated in the heart of Asia in the course of time found that their limited area could not furnish sustenance for so dense and numerous a population, that necessity drove them out in every direction to search for new fields for settlement.

These pressing needs, and actuated by a love of conquest, they at one time flooded Europe and the north of Africa; led their hordes through Siberia, and planted them upon the icy coast of North America, which latitude is ever inimical to the dark-complexioned races, and by an easy course of descent they would gradually drift to the warm and congenial climate of Mexico, and thence by the Central American route to the attractive slopes of the Andes.*

* According to the traditions of the Ayrmares, the leading Peruvian race, there was a time when war and dissension were the ruling traits, and every tribe was sunk in the lowest depths of barbarism. "From

No tribe of Indians yet known to man, save those of whom we speak, possessed that degree of intelligence and that spirit of enterprise as is exemplified in the magnificent structures that once dotted the adopted land of this comparatively extinct race. Lofty temples of hewn stone, with arched corridors grand in proportions, ornamented with sculptured stones and beauti-

---

this condition they were rescued by their tutelar divinity, the Sun, who sent down his own children to reform and instruct them. These were Manco Capac, and his sister and wife, Mama Oello Huaco, who made their appearance on an island in Lake Titicaca, whence under divine instruction they journeyed northward to the spot where the city of Cuzco, which afterwards became the capital of the Incas, now stands. Here they collected together the neighboring savage hordes, and while Manco Capac instructed the men in agriculture and the arts, and inspired them with ideas of social and civil organization, Mama Oello taught the women to spin and weave, and inculcated modesty, grace, and the domestic virtues. From this celestial pair the Incas claimed their descent, in virtue of which they were the high-priests of religion and the heads of the state. In this tradition we trace only another version of the civilization common to all primitive nations, and that imposture of a celestial relationship whereby designing rulers and cunning priests have sought to secure their ascendency among men. Manco Capac is the almost exact counterpart of the Chinese Fohi, the Hindoo Buddha, the terrestrial Osiris of Egypt, the Quetzalcoatl of Mexico, and Votan of Central America. . . . Aside, however, from all traditions, there are monumental evidences that, anterior to the foundation of the Peruvian Empire, there existed on the islands and shores of Lake Titicaca a people of relatively high civilization, the story of whose migration to the northward is probably preserved in a figurative form in that of Manco Capac and his sister; and it may safely be assumed that this people, in their relationships, and in virtue of their intelligence, arrogated to themselves a superiority over the tribes which they brought under their control, and founded an exclusive and aristocratic caste, the Inca race."—*American Cyclopœdia.*

fully-carved wood, and adorned with mosaic-work and hieroglyphic painting, indicating an enlightenment of no ordinary kind, and a familiar acquaintance with Oriental literature; and in that tropic land are found the sculptured idols before whom they bowed and worshiped; and a beautiful road paved with white rock, leading from Kabah to Uxmal, ten inches high and eight feet wide, is pointed out at this late period by the natives, on which the couriers traveled from city to city, conveying written messages from the nobles of one city to the other, and these messages inscribed upon the skins of animals and the bark of trees. These records came to us in part by the traditions common to the present aborigines of the country, and authenticated by the testimony of reliable travelers who have explored this region, and report facts that have passed under their immediate observation. And these unmistakable evidences of superior enlightenment exhibited in the ancient homes of the Toltecan tribes forbid even a reasonable doubt as respects the position that they should take among the nations of earth, being more intelligent, more refined; and corresponding physical conformation allies them forever with the original Mongolian of the East.

Reverting again to the ancient seats of the Mongolian race, it is astonishing what apparent progress this people has made in passing ages; taking into consideration the link which they form in the great chain of races, the last and highest type of the pre-adamic creation, we are enabled to trace the progressive system and the gradually ascending series in the divine programme of God's eternal purpose.

The negro, the Malay, and the American Indian had served their day, and taken their respective positions in the progressive series of original creation, when the Mongolian is introduced, preparatory to the ushering in of a higher and a nobler type of the human species, not perfect in his nature, tarnished in his complexion, yet far superior in mental endowments to any preceding family which had made its *début* on the arena of life, and the only race whose form of government is assimilated to that of a still more refined and enterprising people.* As with the Toltec of Central America, so with the inhabitant of Central Asia. The great wall that bounds China on the north is one of the remarkable wonders of the world; its height is twenty-four feet, and length fifteen hundred miles, and sufficiently broad for two carriages to be driven along abreast from one end to the other. It was constructed several hundred years before the Christian era, for the purpose of checking the invasions of adjacent tribes descended from the same parental stock; a very conclusive argument that no material change has taken place in the government of this empire from the established principle in the political economy of nations, that the moment that all the wealth and resources of a people are concentrated in the hands of the few, by taxation, tyranny, and oppression, it is then that the government becomes centralized, and the liberties and the entire resources of the country become vested in and subject to the will of

* Buckle says, "In Central America extensive excavations have been made, and what has been brought to light proves that the national religion was like that of India, a system of complete and unmitigated terror."

one man, who rules his subordinates with the same discipline exercised by a military commander over his immediate staff. Consequently, tyranny of the darkest hue takes possession of the person and energies of the whole nation, and makes them subservient to the *ipse dixit* of the exacting despot. Such a state of affairs now obtains in the Chinese Empire and with the moguls of the East, and has existed throughout Asia ages upon ages before tradition even had its birth. China boasts the largest canal in the world, together with temples and public buildings that excite astonishment in European and American minds. They have arts and claim a knowledge of the sciences which are yet unknown to us, and we must admit that they have been and still are in possession of secrets which the world has not been able to obtain. They are called civilized, but nevertheless extremely barbarous in many practices sanctioned by law and upheld by the general will of the people. In many respects they are savage and uncompromising in their nature, and devoted to the idolatrous worship which has come down to them from the antediluvian period. The Asiatic Mongols have their libraries containing books on various subjects, and were acquainted with the art of printing in their peculiar way long before Europe made the discovery, and some of them claim that their government was founded many centuries before Commodore Noah embarked on his first sailing-voyage. In examining the literature of India, we find statements there which require a considerable stretch of the imagination to grasp and fully retain, though pregnant with improbabilities far beyond the reach of our credulity; yet the charges of unbelief brought to bear against our authentic historical records by some new-discovered race would provoke within us a smile at the ignorance of these new and unlettered judges of ancient history. The same view no doubt obtains with the Hindoo and John Chinaman when ridicule is thrust at their long-cherished records. They claim for the average life of ordinary men of old only eighty thousand years, and that those who were clothed with sacerdotal robes, and holy in their lives, were permitted to enjoy one hundred thousand years of blissful usefulness on this mundane sphere. Some survived longer, others shorter periods. They go so far as to mention the names of some of their great men who were blessed with such longevity. A king, whose name is Yudhisthir, had the glorious privilege of sitting upon his throne and dispensing justice for the short term of twenty-seven thousand years; while another, called Alarka, wore his crown and was in active duty for the space of sixty-six thousand years. And these great men were unfortunately cut down in the prime of life, for in the Asiatic researches it is recorded, and piously believed by the present inhabitants of the East, that two of their bards, by name Valmic and Vyasa, whose birthdays were separated by a period of eight hundred and sixty-four thousand years, yet that aged and this youthful poet had sat down together and conversed in regard to matters that pertained to the long annals of the past.* Their great collection of laws denominated

* The most remarkable case is that of a very shining character in Oriental history, who united in his person the functions of a king and a saint. "He was the first king, first anchorite, and first saint, and is

the "Institutes of Menu," to which the Hindoo is so much attached, by the best native authorities these great laws were revealed by Heaven to these ancient devotees full two thousand millions of years before Warren Hastings crushed this people with the iron car of avarice. And when China's vaults and Japan's labyrinths of mystic lore are opened up to the vulgar gaze of the Anglo-Saxon, we may read of Antediluvia as the pastime of to-day, and mark on Adam's brow the tint of evening's twilight, and search for antiquity among the mysterious oracles which the morning zephyrs strew promiscuously in the subterranean caverns of the Cumæn Sibyl, and point back to the hour when the sweet influences of Pleiades and Orion cast their mellowed light over the lifeless form of chaotic nature.

---

therefore entitled Prathama-Rajah, Prathama Bhicshacara, Prathama Jina, and Prathama Tirthancara. At the time of his inauguration as king his age was two million years. He reigned six million three hundred thousand years, and then resigned his empire to his sons; and having employed one hundred thousand years in passing through the several stages of austerity and sanctity, departed from this world on the summit of a mountain named Ashtapada."—*Asiatic Researches*, vol. ix. p. 305.

CHAPTER X.

THE CAUCASIAN.

"But man he made of angel form erect,
To hold communion with the heavens above,
And on his soul impressed his image fair,
His own similitude of holiness,
Of virtue, truth, and love."—POLLOK.

THE fifth and last race which engrosses our attention is man, the child of Adam, and the lineal descendant of Shem, Ham, and Japhet, of whom alone the Bible speaks, and who alone is made in God's own image and likeness. The Indo-European, or Caucasian, has a different shaped head from any of the other races; his skull is more oval or elliptical, and is more symmetrical in form. There is no excessive prominence or undue flattening or compression on the top of the head, which invariably manifests itself with all of the lower races; the head is rounder and the forehead broad and full, with the cranial cavity largely developed; marked with a fullness of the forehead and elevation of the brow in accordance with the size of the face, indicating higher intellectual powers rather than indicative of the brutal or sensual.

The facial angle is larger than in any of the other races, and the cranial cavity consequently more fully developed, where are seated the organ of sense, which accounts for the vast difference in the intellectual and progressive capacity of this race over all others, and is illustrated by the fact, that wherever the white man has essayed to establish a supremacy over his inferiors, under reasonable auspices, he has thus far never failed to consummate his ends; for the time by the dint of numbers he has been overpowered, as brute force for a season will triumph over the intellectual advancement, but sooner or later the shackles of enthrallment fall to the ground in the presence of a higher order of genius, wisdom assumes her sway, and the noble attributes of the white man become master of the situation. The Mongols of the East came upon Europe "like a wolf on the fold," and for a time spread darkness over the fair fields of the Indo-European, and now the Magyar of Hungary has, in a measure, been absorbed by the superior race which surrounds him; and the Ottoman Empire hangs like a ragged garment on the confines of Russia, and the dark element once dominant in the Spanish peninsula has succumbed to the genius of true civilization and moral enlightenment, and the Pillars of Hercules may rise out of the ocean and stand as an everlasting monument of the inferiority of the one and the superiority of the other. America can well attest the proud achievements of the European over the savage demons that peopled the western continent. And Western Asia, once the seat of learning and of science and civilization, and where the Star of Bethlehem first threw its radiant light over the broken hopes of a perishing world, is now overrun by the mixed races of the Mongolian and the descendants of

Ishmael, who in hybridizing improve in the physical type, and degrade in the moral and intellectual, until the baser instincts of man assume undivided sovereignty over the heart, and fitly prepare him for the Moslem's work of desecration and destruction. The unsullied Caucasian sought a permanent home beyond the Bosphorus from the devouring hordes that swept across the continent of Asia, and the few who were of necessity left behind have become assimilated in manners, customs, and blood with the dominant race, who first came among them like the avalanche from the summit of the Himalaya Mountains. With this exception, however, that many of the descendants of Abraham as nomad Arabs are still perfect in cranial formation and purity of color, with no alloy of degenerate blood, who have not bowed the knee to the aggressive Mongolian, either to become allied by consanguinity or to pay tribute as a conquered vassal. Mount Caucasus* points her summit to the clouds, and bids defiance to the Mongolian and Sclavonic races. Who would essay to strip her free-born sons of their dear-bought liberties? and is it possible that the advocate of the One-Race dogma would attempt to sully the name of the fair Caucasian by charging upon this race an admixture of Mongolian blood? Such ideas are advanced upon the general declaration that of one blood God created all the nations of the earth. This language was spoken by the Apostle Paul, and was addressed to the Greeks,

* The white camellia, one of the most beautiful of cultivated flowers, is so closely blended with Mount Caucasus in the minds of the southern people, that it has become sacred as the emblem of purity, and eminently representative of the Adamic race.

lineal descendants of Japhet, as found in Acts xvii. 24–26: "God that made the world and all things therein, seeing that he is Lord of heaven and earth, dwelleth not in temples made with hands; neither is worshiped with men's hands, as though he needed any thing, seeing he giveth to all life, and breath, and all things; and hath made of one blood* all nations of men for to dwell on all the face of the earth, and hath determined the times before appointed, and the bounds of their habitation." In the first place, Paul's remarks were addressed directly to the enlightened Athenian, a type of the true Caucasian. Nor is there any evidence that any one of Christ's apostles ever preached the gospel to either of the inferior races, and if they did, there are many plausible reasons to assert that their preaching to them was as the sounding brass or tinkling cymbal. Again, the constituent parts of the blood of vertebrated animals are found by analysis to differ in no particular essential points; in fact, not varying in the component particles more nor less than is observable in the blood of different individuals of the same race. In truth, it is established by the learned in the medical world, that the blood of the same individual undergoes material changes in making its regular circuit through the arterial and venous channels; and again, the blood of the same individual undergoes various changes at various ages of the same party under equal circumstances of health and sobriety. Likewise is the blood altered in its constituent composition by

---

*Luke wrote this gospel, and not Paul, and in none of Paul's epistles is to be found any parallel passage or expression.

a change of food and diet to that extent that the herbivorous feeder may be easily detected from the carnivorous species. And there is also a marked difference observable in the blood of the sanguineous and lymphatic subjects of the white race. And these varied changes must ever continue in the human system, and in the physical economy of man, just as we discriminate the different waters that flow from the bosom of the earth, the one stream is impregnated with minerals and alkalies differing from others in the same vicinity. Therefore, if this scriptural passage is to be interpreted on a scientific basis, then "hath God made of one blood all the nations of the earth, and hath before appointed the bounds of their habitations," to wit, He hath located the negro in Africa, south of the Great Desert; the Malay along the belt of the tropics, and the Mound-builder on the American continent; the Mongolian under the rising sun, and man, the true image of his Creator, on the fertile shores of the Tigris and Euphrates.

If it were possible for man to change his own features, the unguent pores of his body, the color of his skin, flatten his nose, compress his skull, and otherwise disfigure and degrade his perfect type of nobility, tell me why there were no negroes found on the American continent when first discovered. We have an equatorial sun, whose parching rays fall in perpendicular lines upon as arid districts as the original home of the blackest African; we have lakes and seas and oceans that reflect back the concentrated rays of the fiery orb of day; we have sands and plains and jungles and torrid fires to furnish all the elements necessary to generate the black and odoriferous spawn who lords it to-day over the rich heritage of the Semitic race. If food and habit and savage manners and climatic influences and fondness for human flesh, if tornadoes and volcanic floods and devouring earthquakes can fright the human heart and alter the physical formation of man, and change the noblest work of God into the degraded specimen who rears his earth-born savage frame and feature before intelligent man and claims social equality, then ought America to have claimed the proud and exalted privilege of originating one pure unalloyed and unadulterated negro, that he might present himself to the world as a living and a moving ensample of the creative genius or the debasing influence of the virgin soil of America. If there were no other arguments in favor of the plurality of the races, this alone ought to establish the truth of our theory beyond the peradventure of a reasonable doubt.

CHAPTER XI.

HYBRIDITY, COLOR, AND SELECTION.

"If the wild winds seem more drear
Than man's cold charities below,
Behold around his peopled plains,
Where'er the social savage reigns,
Exuberance of woe."—CAMPBELL.

I AM willing to admit that there is only the semblance of an argument in favor of a unity of the human species in the established laws governing the hybridity of the vegetable and animal kingdoms; that hybrid races, originating in the sexual intercourse of entirely different species, do not always as a general rule tend to self-perpetuation. This may apply with apparent force to the brute creation, but can have no bearing in reference to the progeny derived from a cross of the human family.

The intellectual feature of the genus homo predominates over the vegetable and the brute formations, and the natural affinities of the intellectual being are more harmonious, as respects congeniality of feeling, sentiment, and selection; and the repulsive elements that are at work with the instinctive genius of the brute tribes, derived from apprehension, may bring about results entirely different, and not at all attendant upon subjects of higher intellectual capacity, who are operating under preconceived notions of comparative congeniality, where a uniform will has been exercised to the action of a joint selection on the part of both subjects.

In the vegetable kingdom there can be no exercise of will or choice when impregnation ensues; a result exclusively emanating from a fixed law of nature, but superinducing in plants greater production and prolificacy wherever the experiment has been thoroughly tested. The mare (the female of the horse) ordinarily will not yield to the demands of the ass until teased by the male of her own species; nor is there harmonious intercourse between the lion and the tiger, and other carnivorous and herbivorous animals. There must ever exist among these diverse species and discordant natures the apprehension of fear, a foreboding of bodily injury, much akin to the dreadful shock experienced by the chaste of our own race when made to succumb to the violent efforts of the ravisher, to which the chaste victim does not respond by conception; whereas, on the other hand, the brute does conceive and brings forth a monster which is neither fish nor fowl; and a few of these crosses are seldom known to breed with hybrids of the same class, although they propagate occasionally with either of their parental stock, and in the course of time lose their identity almost entirely.

In speaking of animals as respects species, we assume as a basis that those are distinct which have preserved their identity and have remained unchanged during the space of forty-five hundred years, which carries us back anterior to the time of Noah's deluge, according to the chronological computation of Archbishop Usher, which was 2349 years B.C. Dogs have often been represented on the monuments of Egypt as early as the fourth dynasty, 3400 years B.C. So have specimens of the wolf, hyena, and jackal been delineated on the same monuments, and later, down to the eleventh and twelfth dynasties, 2100 to 2400 years B.C.

We find them frequently repeated on the walls of these memorable sepulchres as large as life and perfectly accurate in description, and presenting them every way the fac-simile of the same species now found in the neighboring countries of Asia and Africa.

The greyhound was known long prior to the days of Abraham. So were the pointer, the hound, the bulldog, and the turnspit, together with the wild dog of the woods. And it may seem strange to the cursory reader that the crowned heads of Egypt should have devoted time and means to have these minor animals represented upon their monuments. In every age history informs us that the royal court has unbended its frown and sought the forest to regale a season in the chase of the wild boar and the stag, and the triumphant victor returns from his royal park with the trophies of the chase and depicts upon the spacious walls the flying stag and the pursuing canines, with the same zest that he would inscribe those captives who grace his returning chariot from some foreign field of blood. It is difficult to say from whence came the following animals, as history does not define the dog, the horse, hog, sheep, and goat. As far as we can trace them back, they were known then as distinct as they are found to-day; whether they were original species or distinct genera, or are really hybrids, must ever remain a matter of doubt, but we assume that they are and ever have been distinct. It has been tested and tried satisfactorily that the dog crossed with the wolf or the fox, that this hybrid offspring emanating from either one or the other will not only breed with the parent stock, but are prolific among themselves. And there are many instances on record where they prove to be more prolific in fact than their parents. And natural history is not silent in regard to the sheep* and goat. They are as distinct apparently as any animals found in nature; and wherever coupled together, they are remarkable for prolificacy, both with the parent stock and among themselves. This is also true of the male sheep† and the doe (Cervus capriolus). The same is proverbially true of the three different species of the camels,‡ among themselves, as also with the dromedaries, which are distinct. The one coupled with the other produces hybrids which are long-lived and prolific; the camel with the dromedary, and *vice versa.*

It is unnecessary to enumerate other examples, if it can be established in one instance that hybrids are prolific *inter se* and with the parent stock, which has been done conclusively with regard not only to different species but distinct genera. The scientific inquirer should be satisfied, and the skeptic convinced, that there is a plurality of races among the above-enumerated animals, and that there is nothing unnatural in the productions of the hybrid races of the human family.

There can be no greater cross in nature than that

---

* Molina and Chevreul. † Hellenius.

‡ Linnæus and Cuvier.

arising between the goat and the sheep, and the white man and the negress; and if the progeny of the one is prolific, the other is likewise. And barrenness among hybrids is rather an exception than a rule, and this question of hybridity and productiveness would never have agitated the public mind to the same extent only as a plausible theory to establish the unity of the races.

There is one thing very remarkable with the hybrid classes of the genus homo wherever found on this habitable globe, in any latitude or in any climate, immaterial by whom surrounded, whether by barbarous, half-civilized, or intelligent and moral communities. They are ever destitute and devoid of honesty, virtue, and chastity. There is but one race among whom is practiced strict moral honesty in their daily intercourse with their fellow-men, and whose females are truly and strictly chaste in the highest signification of the term, both honest and chaste from principle and not as a matter of policy; and this high and exalted premium can be alone awarded to the Caucasian family. The African and Polynesian explorer, the Oriental traveler, and the Rocky-Mountain trapper, tell us that true virtue is unknown among the aboriginal races. There are isolated cases of chastity among the varied tribes of earth; but it is the exception rather than the rule, and it obtains alone where vengeance hangs like the sword of Damocles in threatening attitude over the wayward victim. Now, throw into this caldron of corruption the blood of the white man, and the progeny derived from the negro becomes a mulatto; intellectually, we admit that the stock is improved, but the virtue of the one has been destroyed by the leaven of the other, and so on *ad infinitum* as regards all others of the inferior races; so long, at least, as this degenerate taint is visible in feature and formation.

If I am not correct in the assumed premises of a want of true virtue in the mongrel races, then tell us why the Eastern harems are guarded by eunuchs and other imbeciles. The thought is father to the deed; and the custom so prevalent in the East, of veiling the females from the gaze of the world and excluding them from male society, is proof positive of a want of confidence in their virtue, and to avoid an exposure to the seductive influences of the artful, which must always prove the victor over the weaker vessel, whose constitutional tendency at best is to stray from the paths of rectitude.

Color in the human skin is derived from pigment-cells which are mingled with the ordinary epidermic cells; the former of which secrete a black pigment which bears a close relation with that inky fluid for which the cuttle-fish is so much noted, and contains a very large proportion of carbon. These pigment or coloring cells in the epidermis are alone observable in the negro and other dark-skinned races, except in freckles and in the dark spots around the nipples of the fairer race.

The varied hues of complexion met with in the different colored races is due to the number of these cells and to the particular tint of the pigment therein secreted; hence arise the jet-black, brown, copper-colored, olive, and white complexions, that mark the distinctness of complexion characteristic of the human family. And it is urged with great tenacity that these results are brought about by climatic influences, combined with the action of heat and light and the force of sexual selection. A strange theory indeed, that these influences would completely metamorphose the entire physical structure and warp the ennobling attributes of our nature, and so debase our moral being that man completely loses his identity and becomes assimilated in instinct and physiological organization with the quadrumana tribes. And the hypothesis that the jet-black negro, in making his selection for a companion in life, truly prefers one of his own color in preference to those of a lighter hue, is an egregious error, and well supported by the history of the blacks in America, in Hayti, and elsewhere. Having been a slave-owner myself, and a willing resident in their midst for forty years, I speak from my own knowledge of facts, that the jet-black negro almost invariably admires and essays to marry those having brighter skins, while the lighter-complexioned negroes or mulattoes entertain notions of pride as respects color, and are not willing to lower their status by intermarrying with one of a darker hue. And where a mulatto illegitimate turns up in a family of blacks, it becomes the universal favorite of young and old. White is the popular complexion as regards beauty and sprightliness; consequently it is coveted in a high degree by the unvarnished black. Witness the spirit of envy and the deadly hate entertained and fostered by the negroes in Saint Domingo, where has been waged for years a war of extermination against every negro whose complexion showed an admixture of the Caucasian blood. To be a mulatto in that island was a matter of no congratulation to the hybrid; because it was a mark of superiority intellectually and as a gallant, and necessarily brought upon him the vengeance of his less fortunate black neighbor.

It is as natural for the negro to ape the white man as it is for the monkey to ape his superior. The converse of the proposition, where is the full-grown Caucasian that will debase his or her lineage by amalgamation with the black sons or daughters of Africa? If this be the programme, then, fair reader, remember that the hour is not far distant when the American mind will become reconstructed on the subject of miscegenation. And the very descendants of those who would now demoralize human society by an advocacy of such heresies, will be the first to persecute and thrust down the deluded individual whose blood is tinged with that of the negro. Voluntary sexual selection on the part of man, as producing degeneracy of character and debasement of physical structure, is a humbug practically speaking; or else, as before stated, America in the days of Columbus should have presented to the world so remarkable a prodigy as the full-fledged negro. Selection in violation of the laws of consanguinity, if persisted in, will invariably produce idiocy, and at the same time result in physical deformity, to the mortification of him who indulges in such revolting practices. In fact, no law of nature can be violated with impunity, and intelligent mortals must pay the penalty in every instance for every deviation from the standard of right. What a farce is presented to the mind in the doctrine of selection, where an individual by choice selects a partner with a flat nose or a long heel, and this idiosyncrasy becomes a family failing through endless generations, until the flat-nose becomes a family characteristic, and the leg of each son and daughter becomes located in the centre of the foot, as is nearly the case with some specimens of the African type!

On the monuments of the Eastern hemisphere the Caucasian, Mongol, and negro are found distinct in all the features that mark the original races for the space of nearly three thousand years before the Christian era, to which I shall allude again at its proper place.

There is a strong hypothesis afloat in the world that Shakspeare favored the doctrine of miscegenation in his memorable play of Othello; which is altogether erroneous. For about this period the black race was regarded as only fit subjects to become slaves in the newly-settled colonies of America, a fact practically executed by England, Spain, and Portugal. And Shakspeare, in his selection, takes the noblest specimen of the dark-visaged race, Othello, who was to marry the daughter of the respected senator of Venice. He was brave, intelligent, and of manly form and demeanor. Desdemona was a woman of some intelligence, but of coarse habits of mind, who was moving in high society, but that society was corrupt and depraved. And a morbid appetite in connection with a spirit of romance, originating from the demoralization* so common in Southern Europe at this epoch, actuated and urged her forward to marry this Moor, which to

* The intelligent reader remembers Lord Byron's attachment to the Countess of Guiccioli, which was not very creditable to either. In the mean time civilization had materially advanced in the south of Europe.

her brought death, and to her family mortification and disgrace; a sad commentary upon the frailty of human nature.

This Moor was not a negro, but a cross of the Mongolian with the nomad races of Western Asia; but inferior to the Indo-European in all the attributes that make the man.

Shakspeare detested this alliance. And the moral of this tragedy will go down to the latest generation as a warning to the Desdemonas, victims of the sickly sentimentality of our present school of philosophy.

CHAPTER XII.

CHILDREN OF HAM NOT NEGROES.—SETTLEMENT OF EGYPT.

> "His art and honors wouldst thou seek
> Embossed on grandeur's giant walls,
> Or hear his moral thunders speak
> Where senates light their airy halls."
>
> CAMPBELL.

I WILL now revert to Noah and his family after escaping the perils of the deluge. To support his family he turned his attention to the tillage of the ground, and planted a vineyard, and drank too freely of the wine, and became intoxicated and lay uncovered in his tent, which being observed by his son Ham, he ridiculed the old gentleman in the presence of his two brothers. Gen. ix. 24–27: "And Noah awoke from his wine, and knew what his younger son had done unto him. And he said, Cursed be Canaan; a servant of servants shall he be unto his brethren. And he said, Blessed be the Lord God of Shem; and Canaan shall be his servant. God shall enlarge Japheth, and he shall dwell in the tents of Shem; and Canaan shall be his servant."

I have quoted this passage of Scripture with a view to explain away the error, which many intelligent thinkers have fallen into, as respects the servitude of the negro, and to disabuse the mind of the false notion entertained that Ham was the father of the negro race. Neither Canaan nor any of his descendants ever located in Southern or Central Africa, the home of the genuine black man prior to the days of Herodotus, which was 500 years B.C. And two thousand five hundred years anterior to this date the negro, as described by us and known as such to-day, was familiar to the Egyptians, the latter of whom were the lineal descendants of the Hamitic race.

Read the history of Canaan, the son of Ham, in Gen. x. 15–17: "And Canaan begat Sidon his first-born, and Heth, and the Jebusite, and the Amorite, and the Girgasite, and the Hivite," etc.

These tribes every Bible-reader knows occupied the land of Canaan, or Palestine; that beautiful country flowing with milk and honey, which the Lord gave to the Israelites when he brought them forth out of the land of Egypt, 1491 years B.C. And the Lord directed his chosen people to destroy the last vestige of these tribes, old and young, that no remnant of them or their idolatrous worship might remain to contaminate and defile his people. Joshua, however, spared many of them, and made covenants with them, to the effect that they should be hewers of wood and drawers of water unto all the congregation of the house of Israel. And they were bondsmen, the servant of servants, unto the Israelites for many generations: a literal fulfillment of the Noachic prophecy, which was never intended to have any bearing upon the negro, his location, origin, or bondage.

As early as 1500 B.C. there appears in ancient Thebes a tableau selected from the celebrated monument of Seti-Meneptha, or as better known, Belzoni's tomb, one of the kings of the nineteenth dynasty. So early as this date had the Egyptians divided mankind into four distinct species, whom they classed as Red, Yellow, Black, and White; the latter representing themselves as being superior to all other races, showing that they were not ignorant of the diversities of mankind. And innocently have they furnished us these portraits as an evidence of the fact that the curse pronounced upon Canaan had no connection with the Ethiopian of modern times.

The Ethiopia* of the Bible was included in what is known now as Central or Upper Egypt. And sometimes a portion of Arabia, bordering on the Red Sea, was also called Ethiopia. And remember not to con-

---

* In the poems of Homer it is divided into Eastern and Western Ethiopia, the Red Sea making the division. Herodotus and the later Greek and Roman geographers also repeat this distinction, and refer to a sun-burnt face, from *αιθω*, to burn, and *οψ*, the countenance, and not to a negro.

found Ethiopia of the Bible with the present geographical Ethiopia, or Negro-land, of which I shall speak in due time.

Egypt derived its name from Ham, the son of Noah, and it is frequently called the land of Ham in the book of Psalms.* Mizraim and Cush, two of Ham's sons, located in the land of Egypt; the one near the mouth of the Nile, and the other higher up on the same river. The territory occupied by the one geographers gave the name of Egypt, and to the other Ethiopia, which along the fertile banks of the Nile did not extend for ages over five degrees of latitude, or about three hundred miles, and the Romans say at no period did civilization extend farther up the Nile than to 19° of north latitude.

And to impress upon the mind the character of Ham's descendants. Nimrod, who was a son of Cush, began to be a mighty man upon the earth, and, as Moses writes, was a mighty hunter before the Lord. Nor did he confine himself to the chase of wild beasts alone, but extended his conquests over man, and made him entirely subservient to his will, and through his supremacy of intellect and domineering spirit he founded the great city of Babylon, and attempted to erect the noted tower of Babel, which brought upon the inhabitants thereof that confusion which dispersed the post-diluvians, and sent them into the four corners of the world to select permanent homes. Nimrod is supposed to have remained at Babylon with his imme-

* Psalm cv. 23: "Israel also came into Egypt; and Jacob sojourned in the land of Ham." Making Egypt synonymous with the land of Ham.

diate family; and with his adherents he established this city as the capital of the Assyrian Empire. While others of the same line, proceeding under the spirit of discovery, cast their habitations on the alluvion or Delta of the Nile, and which since has proven to be the rich granary of the world. When Cush and Mizraim essayed to emigrate to this portion of Africa, the probabilities are greatly in favor of the theory that the negro was unknown to our Western Asiatics, and that the nigrition type of the genus homo was still confined to Interior and Southern Africa. The Mongolian* of the East, however, had made his appearance on the borders of the Tigris and Euphrates, and had contributed his share of labor in constructing the noble temples and palaces that were occupied by Nebuchadnezzar and others of the Assyrian kings;† as in aftertimes the negro was brought from Lake Tsad and the head-waters of the Nile, and made to contribute his quota of muscle and might in constructing those lofty pyramids which are the wonder and admiration of every

---

* The Mongolian at this period occupied that portion of Africa lying north of the Great Desert. (The Sahara or Great Desert at this epoch was an inland sea.) They also inhabited a greater part of the continent of Europe, which in the course of time was surrendered to the Indo-European.

† "Now there is a vast mass of evidence pointing to an early population of Western Asia by a race kindred in many respects to that which we now call Turanian. Such a race certainly possessed the highlands of Elam, between lower Mesopotamia and the table-land of Iran, the ancient Media; and its traces have been found in Chaldea itself, on the monuments where records have been recently deciphered. There was, too, an universal tradition of an occupation of Western Asia by the Scythians, that is, the Turanian race."—PHILIP SMITH, vol. i. p. 195.

age. Superior intellect and the aggregation of wealth subdued the masses and built mausoleums in honor of despotism.

Then tell us not that Cush or Mizraim or Ham or Nimrod is the progenitor of the negro. They in fact first utilized the negro and converted him into a machine for agricultural and architectural purposes. And let me impress it with vivid letters upon the mind of the reader, that this degraded race was instrumental in hastening the decline and fall of this proud and illustrious people, as here again are the first symptoms of sexual intercommunication since the deluge between the high-born and ignoble races, which utterly debased the original Egyptian, and brought upon this beautiful, this lovely country, the prophetic vengeance of an incensed Jehovah, which in the due course of revolving ages was fulfilled to the most literal interpretation of the prophecy. The inspired author* denounces terrible curses upon Egypt and upon all the mingled† races of that and of neighboring states; and, furthermore, declares that the land of Egypt shall cease to be ruled by her own princes and become the basest of nations.

The Egyptians have been regarded as the most intelligent of all the ancient nations. History at an early period gave them a prominence for wisdom, learning, and a familiarity with the arts and sciences unsurpassed by all other kingdoms of the earth, and from whom the Israelites, the Grecians, and other surrounding nations copied. The invention of alphabetical letters and the art of writing came originally from the Egyp-

* Ezekiel, chaps. xxix. and xxx. † Ezekiel, chap. xxx. 5.

tians. And Moses states that in mystic lore they were not excelled by any people under the sun. Their proficiency in the arts and sciences, and the exemplification of civilization and progress found here among the descendants of Ham, dates back as early as the kings of the fourth dynasty, 2450 years B.C.,—the monuments of this period show the advances that had been made; the masonry of their buildings, and the sculpture of the human form, together with their habits and manners of life, attest their ingenuity and their claims to civilization and refinement. And this we must remember was at a period in Egyptian history before the blood of the negro and the Mongolian had infused itself into the veins of the Hamitic race.

The ablest ethnologists who credit the races with one origin progress admirably well in locating the descendants of Noah, until an effort is made to people Central Asia and Africa, and to account for the diverse physical changes now perceptible in every quarter of the globe. In solving this proposition, they become so thoroughly mystified that the wisest strategy cannot relieve them from the dilemma, which Philip Smith, one of the happiest delineators of this subject, admits in the following words: "This question is one of the most difficult in the whole science of ethnology;" and proceeding a little further, he admits that "the ancient language of Egypt, and the Coptic derived from it, have perhaps the best claim to represent the Hamitic family; but it is now clear that both the people of Egypt and their language contained a large infusion of nigrition (or negro) element." Though Egypt was originally pure and unsullied with the blood of the inferior races, and so long as she remained thus exempt, her position among the nations of earth was without a rival. Her armies were triumphant on every field and on every sea, and the scholars of every nation came within her borders to learn wisdom and to pay homage to her sovereigns, and her great superiority was acknowledged by all the kingdoms of the world. Warlike encroachments upon the territory of the negro soon brought this supple element to contribute to the growing wealth of Egypt, until, in the course of time, the peculiar animal worship of the negro was introduced into those Nilotic cities and embraced by the people at large as the national religion of the whole country. The serpent-, the crocodile-, and the vermin-worship to which the entire nation had become addicted at the epoch of the exodus of the Israelites, only manifests the outcropping of voudouism, the diabolic snake-worship so prevalent among the besotted inhabitants of Ethiopia proper. This base devotion of serpent-worship* has not been obliterated from the minds of the lower orders of the negroes of the United States, though planted here for over two hundred years amidst the most benign Christian influences. But a short time since, the public mind was shocked and horrified at the thought that the Digby child of New Orleans had been kidnapped and sacrificed on the altar of voudouism. Egypt, to pay this penalty of a violated law, was overrun about 600 years B.C. by Cyrus, the founder of the Persian Empire, and again, one hundred years later, by Xerxes, one of his successors. The advent of the Persians upon

* The serpent has been worshiped by half the known world.

the soil of Egypt is the first introduction of the Mongolian into the land of the Pharaohs which can be established beyond a doubt by historical records. The presumption is, however, favorable, from the nomadic character of this people, that they had long before this period migrated from their native plains, and made inroads into both Europe and Africa. The Chaldeans, some half-century prior to the Medo-Persian conquest, had invaded Egypt, whose armies had been supplied from the same Asiatic district, and contained, in all probability, a similar class of recruits. In fact, the Scythians had made their inroads at various times towards the west, and left the mark of physical demoralization wherever their foot-prints can be traced on the sands of time.

Ancient historical records abound with descriptions of the mongrel races which came like an avalanche from the East and spread themselves over Northern Africa and Europe, and whose overpowering numbers overthrew every opposing barrier, and whose destroying breath, like the simoon of the desert, brought desolation over the rich fields and palatial abodes of civilization and refinement. They are represented as deformed in figure, of squatty stature, large and unproportioned heads, dark-visaged, and of an unearthly appearance; their color varying from a light olive to a dingy brown; their language, manners, and physical make and armor differing in many respects. And they seem to be so little allied to the human race that the writers of that period could only recognize them by their power of speech as being a part of the human family; and their every appearance was so at variance with the general appearance of man, that the ancient historian supposed them to be the progeny of some sorcerers with the demons of the desert.

And in the army of Xerxes, a marked difference was observable in the mixed races which had been thrown together by this indefatigable warrior. For instance, those recruits gathered from the elevated plains of Asia, and those from the Persian provinces bordering India on the south, were each marked by their peculiarity of habit, costume, color, and physical formation: the one partaking more of the Mongolian type of the Eastern Asiatic, and the other assuming the darker visage and osteological idiosyncrasies of the Malayan type of the Indian Archipelago of the south. Both of these differing more or less from the hybrid cross of the Ishmaelite, and utterly dissimilar in every conceivable aspect as to physical conformation, color, and general appearance from the mulattoes and other grades representing that diabolical cross between the true descendants of Ham and the nigrition tribes of Lower Africa. As respects this Hamitic branch, at a later period, the historian declares that the Egyptian is allied by blood and language with both the Turanian and negro races, as is supported by physical qualities, habits, and religion. Their reddish color distinguishes them from both the Caucasian and negro, whereas their thick lips and elongated eye connect them with the black race, and possessing a religious devotion peculiar to the Asiatics, yet thoroughly devoted to the worship of animals, snakes, etc.

The cow has been venerated in India from the most remote antiquity. And the worship of the god Odin,

Woden, Goden, as called by different nations, is the same deity, and had its origin in Central Asia, as also did the worship of the god Buddha, so common in India; and the ceremonial rites of the two are identically the same wherever they prevail. Also from the same quarter of the globe came the worship of the sun, to which luminary the Mexicans paid their religious devotions by sacrificing human beings on the lofty summits of their temples in full view of the adoring multitude beneath,—showing conclusively the origin of the race by a perpetuity of these unholy rites in their long-adopted country. Nor has Asia yet given up this idolatrous devotion, or discontinued her efforts to appease her household deities by the offering of human sacrifices.

Odin, or Woden, synonymous with Buddha, at one period was the tutelar deity of the Druids of Great Britain, and, in fact, of the whole Teutonic or Indo-European race,—a religion practiced by the Greeks and other enlightened nations under the denomination of Mercury, another name for the same deity. The question here arises, How did the Indo-European become imbued with this peculiar form of worship, which more properly belonged to the Central Asiatic? The worship of the sun became the national religion of the Toltecs by the implantation of colonies in that region from the elevated plateau of Asia, they having imbibed and preserved their religion as first received at the hands of their Turanian ancestors, and impressed it afterwards upon the aboriginal inhabitants of the American continent as far as their influence extended, both by fire and sword, as in previous ages did Mahomet and his followers plant the peculiar dogmas of the Koran in the hearts of the vanquished races of Asia and Northern Africa. And by due process of reasoning per force of analogy and common sense, and especially where stubborn facts form the basis of argument as they exist in support of the following theory. That in ancient times, as the crowded masses along the vast plains of Mongolia were perishing for want of supplies to maintain animal life, some daring leader, of Mongolian extraction, or semi-Ishmaelite, or Bedouin wanderer from the great desert of Asia, gathered his myriad hordes from the burning sands of Indus to the frozen shores of Siberia, and from the volcanic isles of Japan to the sacred soil of Palestine, and with an army whose name is myriad, and whose numbers eclipse the sands of the sea-shore,—a motley herd, the denizens of every clime and the commingled blood of every race, whose motto was pillage and plunder and sacrilegious desecration of all that was holy and pure, and led on by some daring leader like Attila of the Huns, or Alaric of the Visigoths,—swept across Western Asia, Northern Africa, and all of Europe, and by force of numbers made every nation tributary to their exactions in point of wealth, habits, and religion. Until, in the course of a few generations, the form of worship practiced throughout Europe, Western Asia, and Northern Africa had undergone, by persecution and oppression on the part of their conquerors, an entire metamorphosis, which resulted in the establishment of this idolatrous worship, which, from custom, became a common fixture in the minds of all classes, until some more daring invader usurped the religious seats of the great Woden, and instituted other rites and devotions in lieu of those which had held these races spell-bound for centuries past.

The limited geographical knowledge of the most enlightened European nations at this early period, and the absence of comparatively all intercourse between neighboring nations, left them in considerable doubt as to what country these various warlike hordes emanated from. A majority, at least, of the ancient historians admit that they came originally from Eastern Asia, occupied and overran at different periods the European continent, and these nomadic tribes passed under the different names of Goths, Ostrogoths, Visigoths, Vandals, and Huns. Fortunately for the cause of civilization and human progress, their reign of supremacy did not last a great while. The Caucasian or Indo-European rose in the power of his might, asserted his wonted superiority, and threw off the barbaric yoke; and, as previously remarked, drove a part of the Mongolian conquerors to the cold climate of Scandinavia, where they eke out a miserable existence in an uncongenial latitude; while a part found a temporary home in the fastnesses of the Pyrenees and the Spanish peninsula, and others, having overrun Egypt and the land of the Carthaginian, finally spread themselves along the southern waters of the Mediterranean or the Great Sea and commingled their corrupt blood with that of the Phœnicians, at one time a pure Semitic tribe, but which by the great sin of miscegenation became demoralized, and forfeited the high position attained by the prowess of her Hannibal, and thereby stained her escutcheon with the foul charge of Punic faithlessness.

Mongolia's dark-visaged sons, in settling along the western and northern coasts of Africa, by intermixture have bleached the nigrition tribes and infused new life into their sluggish veins, while in Hungary and Spain the last remnant of the Scythians are fast disappearing by the slow process of absorption on the part of the more numerous Caucasian. And the glory of the past has departed from the Magyars of Hungary, and the Ottoman Empire, so long upheld by the military prowess of interested nationalities, and yet so feeble from imbecility and corruption, must sooner or later be swallowed up by the Sclavonic race, and cease both in Asia and Europe to have even the semblance of an existence. And wherever upon the broad expanse of nature you find the inferior races occupying fertile or desirable districts of country, which become at any period the object of cupidity on the part of the more intellectual and enterprising Caucasian race, it has been, and ever will be, the fate of that people and of that country to become tributary to the genius of the Indo-European. It is a fixed axiom in the organic law of the universe, that superior intellectuality has and ever will prevail, as much so as falling bodies have a tendency to seek the centre of attraction.

CHAPTER XIII.

THE RELIGION OF THE RACES.

"What are monuments of bravery,
Where no public virtues bloom;
What avails in lands of slavery
Trophied temples, arch, and tomb?"
CAMPBELL.

CARLYLE says that nine millions of human beings have been sacrificed by war and persecution to establish the cross as an emblem of our Christian religion. If such be the case, then we cannot materially err in saying that it required a hecatomb of twenty millions of souls to establish the crescent as the emblem of Mahomet's religious dynasty. This train of thought passes through my mind in reviewing the subject of the religion of the Cross in connection with the various races whose origin and history we have been tracing through these pages; and though my views herein expressed may differ from the published and entertained theories of the nineteenth century, still, in all candor, there is more of truth and less of fiction couched herein than the world may be willing to admit. For the sake of convenience, I shall divide the religious sects or creeds into only three great parties, leaving the minor religious isms of the day entirely out of the question. Then we have the followers of the three creeds,—one of the Bible, and another of the Koran, the residue pagans: God, Mahomet, and the Creature. Intelligent reader, tell us, where does God reign in the vast area of his own creation? and where does the Moslem's creed find its unnumbered millions of blinded devotees? The Caucasian is the only race under the sun that takes the Bible as their rule and guide, for their faith and practice; "and upon this rock I will build my church, and the gates of hell shall not prevail against it." And millions upon millions of treasure are annually expended by the evangelical world for the purpose of proselyting the nations of the earth and converting them to the true religion of the gospel; a noble undertaking, we readily admit, which we sincerely hope may continue to go on until the last vestige of paganism and immorality shall be eradicated from the hearts of the human family. And in all sincerity of soul, what good has thus far been accomplished when the missionary passes beyond the borders of the Caucasian race or the confines of his habitation? Let China and the Indies speak in answer to this interrogatory. The devotion of the Oriental is still fixed upon his ancient gods, and the preaching of the gospel to him is as the sounding brass or the tinkling cymbal.

The holy efforts and the sanguine prayers of the devoted missionary of the Cross have proved unavailing with this idol-adoring people, and ofttimes, as opportunity presented itself, the masses urged on by the subalterns in office and winked at by the lordlings in power, the hue and cry has been raised of "Great is Diana of the Ephesians" against the unfortunate and devoted missionary, who either perished by the executioner's axe or found refuge on board of some friendly vessel in port. The Malayan tribes, as previously remarked, have a passionate fondness for the flesh of the white-faced missionaries of the North; and the red man of the West has a remarkable fondness for the long-flowing scalp of his praying pale-faced brother, with which to ornament his person in the war-dance of his tribe. The negro and the hybrid races, from the Delta of the Nile, along the Mediterranean to the Pillars of Hercules, and on the eastern shores of the Atlantic, and across Central Africa to the Straits of Bab-el-Mandeb, the Moslem's faith is the adopted creed of the mongrel inhabitants. And the unalloyed negro of interior Ethiopia still bows to his same original gods, which Egypt copied and embraced in her early excursions to the land of Nigritia, a sample of which the deluded Israelites carried in their hearts out of the land of Egypt, which became a golden calf in the wilderness of Sinai. And as a penalty for this animal-worship, the fiery serpent was turned loose in the camps of this chosen people, and brought instant death to the sufferer, until the brazen serpent was erected in the midst of the camp and proved a panacea for every ill. For several years the Chinese have been living in our midst on the Pacific coast, and are gradually making their way into the central and eastern States of the Union; and even in this land of Bibles and religious liberty, is there one solitary convert to the doctrines of the Cross among these new emigrants to our fertile shores? And if so, it lacks confirmation in the public mind, and can only be regarded as an exception to the general rule.

It is with the most delicate sense of feeling that I

approach this part of the subject, which treats of the religion of the Cross in connection with the African race as now found in America and her neighboring islands. I do not desire to appear as an arbiter dispensing judgment upon the final destiny of our adopted citizens; the facts, however, I shall not withhold from public scrutiny, but leave every unbiased mind to form its own conclusion. A long and uninterrupted acquaintance and familiarity with this class affords an abundant opportunity to speak of them from the record.

It is proverbial that the ministers of the gospel among this people are noted for dishonesty, and are the instigators of the deviltry which is perpetrated by the pliant instruments of their spiritual leaders. And their so-called gospel lights are the hierarchy which constitute the *summum bonum* of all earthly perfection; the blind actually leading the blind.

Though reared and educated in a land of gospel light, they still cling with avidity to the ancient superstition of their fathers, and assume an importance of religious enlightenment and of gospel knowledge which cannot be corrected by the holy zeal of our wisest divines; and some of them, in utter ignorance of divine truths, stand up before their audiences with a lighted candle resting upon their heads, an emblem of their gifted inspiration in holy law, and harangue their deluded hearers until the fire of nature moves upon the entire congregation, and a pell-mell shout and scuffle pervades the whole mass, when a casual observer would reasonably suppose that the demons from Tartarus were holding their midnight orgies in commemoration of the general judgment.

And though often asserted by the Exeter Hall liberty-loving clique that the negro of the South was debarred the privileges of the Christian religion, such is not the case, nor has it ever occurred to my knowledge in the fair sunny South,—the very contrary has been the practice. The slave was often required to attend Divine service, and intelligent ministers have been employed time and again to preach to this class.

With all the restraints that have been thrown around them, the unaccepted offering of Christianity, the precepts of the holy men of God, the examples of the Christian communities in which they have been raised and the prayer-loving families in which many have been reared, with the same influences operating upon them as were bestowed upon the white children of the same household, yet they have presented a deaf ear to the kind admonition of an educated conscience, and shrink back from the light of the gospel dispensation, and embrace with open arms the heterodox and damning views conjured up by the ignorant and superstitious leaders who essay to be lights and demi-gods of the world. The truth is announced in Heaven's own revealed words, "Thou art weighed in the balances and art found wanting." The Spirit of God will not always strive with his creatures; they are devoted to their idols, and the command has gone forth, "Let them alone." And the time fast approaches that the remnant of this people which shall escape the whirlpool of dissipation, the casualties of time, and the ravages of demoralization, shall sooner or later relapse back into that barbarism from whose bourne no traveler returns. And this, too, is asserted of this race in the face of the truth that no African in his native jungles has yet accepted the gospel privileges, or attained to the high distinctions in religious enlightenment which it has been the good fortune of this class to reap in their newly-adopted American homes. To attempt to evangelize those who have placed themselves beyond the pale of hope is like throwing pearls to swine. Then the question arises in the Christian mind, Are all of these inferior races doomed to destruction by Heaven's unchanging decrees? By no means; they are saved by grace, an immutable principle in the Divine economy. The heathen are not all lost: the impenitent of every nation, together with the scoffer and the blasphemer, whatever may be his language or his race, will most assuredly perish with all the nations that forget God.

The infant and the idiot, with all others who die before they reach the years of accountability, by the inscrutable decrees of Divine Providence are saved by grace, through the atonement made by the Son of God. For the adults there can be no hope, as salvation for them alone comes through faith in the atoning sacrifice, —the only name given under heaven or among men whereby they can be saved. If they reject Him, who, then, can become their deliverer? Redemption is offered free to all mankind, without money and without price; and there can be no fault or blame attached to the inspired truth, where the subject willfully rejects the proffered mercy and builds his hopes upon the traditions of men, or founds them upon any other rock save the chief corner-stone.

CHAPTER XIV.

GEOLOGY.

"The earth's a thief, that feeds and breeds by a composture stolen from general excrement."—SHAKSPEARE.

THOUGH geology is in its infancy, yet the study of this science thus far has brought to light the hidden truths which have lain for unmeasured ages in the unexplored cloisters of mother earth.

The gradual cooling of the earth's surface in the primitive era of her early history is yet marked with indelible lines, and can be traced by the finger of Science with the same accuracy that the telescope marks the position of the different planets in their various orbits, or as the genius of man can command the lightning and utilize it in the daily transactions of life. In the deep bosom of the earth we find the crystallized masses in unstratified beds, showing conclusively the solid state that the surface assumed as the earth gradually parted with its heat. Here, in their natural state, we find the granite, porphyry, and basalt which constitute the basis of the stratified rocks, and upon which foundation are built up the various layers, one upon the other, which have been accumulating age upon age by the gradual disintegration of the surrounding masses. While this vast globe was undergoing the cooling process, the surface originally was comparatively smooth, save where contraction ensued and deep fissures opened wide their gaping mouths, which in time became valleys or natural channels for the flow of water, which in their course united with others and formed brooks and rivers; and they, leading on to other depressions, assumed the magnitude of seas and oceans. In the course of time, by the action of internal fires, convulsions ensued, emanating from the introduction of water and the generation of steam. This unstratified surface was broken up, and upheavals of vast magnitude interspersed the surface of the earth. Hence arose the mountain ranges which traverse the different continents of the globe. Other portions from similar causes became depressed, and the waters retired to their level again and formed other seas and oceans, and the fossilized rocks, which had required myriads of years to form and solidify beneath the depths of the ocean, were thrown up with the primeval unstratified masses, and the granite, with each subsequently formed strata, assumed positions throughout nature far above the level of the sea, and at various dips to the horizon. These convulsions have occurred time and again in remote ages, and have altered the face not only of nature, but changed the position of the original masses, solidified by the cooling process, in such a way that the mind actually becomes bewildered at the vast metamorphosis to which this sublunary sphere has been subjected by the violent commotions of anterior ages.

The mind naturally inquires, Why does science place the granite, porphyry, and basalt as the original exterior of the earth's surface? From the very fact that this outer periphery of the earth's surface was not composed of layers, or strata, but purely crystallized rock, exhibiting evidences of having been subjected to intense heat. And again, no traces of organic remains have ever been found imbedded in these rocks anywhere throughout the globe indicating the existence of living beings, either of the animal or vegetable kingdom. By the gradual disintegration, or wearing away, of the solid rocks of which this world is composed, and the gradual deposition of these minute particles in many portions of the visible globe, the geologist has ascertained beyond the possibility of a doubt that the earth's crust has been raised by these accretions to the full depth or height of eight or ten miles. This fact is established by the various layers or strata overlying each other, as is observable on the margin of streams, where the silent deposit has been made year by year from successive inundations; and in these various strata are found the remains of plants and animals, which successive convulsions of nature have destroyed and thrown in mass and again covered with other deposits of a similar or dissimilar nature, and so on are these various strata marked and identified from the lowest bed of crystallized granite to the alluvion deposit of to-day. The internal fires at different epochs have thrown out untold volumes of lava, which have added their quota in forming these immense deposits, of which Herculaneum and Pompeii must ever remain perpetual yet silent witnesses.

Science informs us that the world has undergone many changes since its creation, concerning which the tradition of man has never given us any reference, the truth of which, however, is thoroughly attested by the book of rocks, in which are buried the extinct remains of plants and animals, ascending gradually one series above the other, period after period, the alliance of the one with the other bearing no similarity, but showing in every respect a distinct origin and a special adaptation to surrounding circumstances,—with the animals, a higher order of advancement, and with the plants, a more luxuriant growth.

These various creations have no doubt flourished in those periods more suitable to their growth, and at a time when the surface and circumambient air were better adapted to support the life of the numerous inhabitants of the globe. The fiat would go forth when God in his providence would sweep from the face of nature the last vestige of the animal and vegetable kingdom, and leave this débris to moulder back to mother earth, whose traces we now read in the deep bowels of the earth; and these decomposing elements again furnish food for new plants and animals distinct in their originality and more perfect in form and structure than those of a former epoch, illustrating conclusively the ascending series in the creative programme of an all-wise Providence.

The first sedimentary stratum, or deposit, is termed Primary, and is several thousands of feet in thickness, and for its formation required ages, comprising possibly millions of years. In this strata we find imbedded vestiges of animal life only, and they of a marine character exclusively, and belonging to the zoophyte family. They were numerous and were scattered over a vast extent of territory, and readily exemplify the wisdom inculcated in the Divine economy, in placing upon this hemisphere such animal life as the crude elements of nature could the better sustain. These are the bivalve, mollusk, and the zoophyte, destitute of sight and hearing, and primitive in their organization. The next strata in course is the Silurian, which contains more numerous remains of the vegetable and animal kingdoms than the one preceding, but still less than is found in the old red sandstone; and so on do we see this progressive increase in quantity, quality, and variety of organic remains, until we reach the more modern or tertiary deposits, where geology discloses again new and distinct varieties, both of animals and plants, imposing one over the other at each successive geological period, until the earth becomes adapted to the full use and enjoyment of man, together with those animals which we find everywhere cotemporary with him; while the preceding inhabitants of earth invariably perish and become food for the sustenance of a higher order of species, and these organic remains become a thorough index to the genealogy of all former existent life, as well as an index to the past chronological history of this world. And this theory does not mar nor can it conflict with Divine revelation as interpreted by theologians of the present hour, that the days of creation were indefinite periods of time, having no reference whatever to the specific days of our own times. Nor does the theory of the gradation of plants and animals as successive creations conflict with Divine revelation, or with the dictates of reason or common sense.

These immense deposits of organic remains, covering

almost the entire surface of the earth, and of a depth in many places exceeding six or eight miles in thickness, must have required such an illimitable number of ages to accomplish such enormous results that the mind wavers in its computation of such vast calculations,—millions upon millions of years. Look at the immense number of rivers that are continually rolling their volumes of muddy water into the great abyss of the ocean; and the highest estimate yet placed by scientific observers upon the accumulations that take place in the bottom of all our seas is one foot in a thousand years. At this rate, when will sufficient time have elapsed to deposit ten miles of sedimentary fossiliferous strata over almost the entire surface of God's creation? Natural causes have thrown up and located these successive deposits in various portions of the globe, and have torn them asunder in every conceivable way, and have introduced through their gaping chasms and fissures the liquid porphyry and granite, and in after-ages other convulsions have sunk again these elevated mountains, hills, and plains to the bottom of the ocean, and in due time have upheaved them again, to become the habitation of a more sublimated animal and vegetable life.

In the upper members of the Silurian, fishes are first discovered of cartilaginous structure entirely, and whose frames are destitute of all bony substance; nor until a later period in geological history do fishes appear with bony skeletons, as also reptiles and the larger mammalia tribes. In fact, the highest order of the vertebrata families in their season take possession of the earth, and leave their foot-prints impressed indelibly upon the tablets of the passing age; for instance, the woolly rhinoceros, hyena, mammoth, and mastodon, and cotemporary with these extinct mammifers also appear the quadrumana tribes, some with and others without tails, who take their position in the fossiliferous rocks in the gradual ascending scale of Divine creation.

England, France, India, and America, each in their turn have brought to light the petrified monkey, and he stands before us as a fossil, the precursor of man, a still higher and nobler species. And truly with great reluctance has the geologist admitted that man has ever been discovered in a fossil state, lest the pre-adamite should appear and be regarded as more ancient than the preconceived opinions of many have ever yet allotted to him; and possibly that such an admission might overturn the cherished dogma of the unity of the human family. Science, however, comes to his relief, and no longer can it be maintained that man is an exception to the general rule.

The last great change in the geological history of the world is denominated the drift, or diluvium period, when animal and vegetable life was destroyed on a large scale, which must have antedated the Noachic deluge many thousands of years. And in this drift or deposit are found the remains of animals, many of which are now extinct. Among the rest here imbedded are the mastodon, elephant, megalonyx, and other of the mammalia tribes. And again, when this great change took place throughout the face of nature, there must also have occurred a change of seasons, corresponding to the evidences contained in the book of rocks. The mammoth and elephant were inhabitants at one period of the frozen regions of Siberia; their remains in some instances are taken from the earth in this cold climate in a state of partial decomposition, while the earth itself still retains in some localities the smell of decaying animal matter. As a great feeder, the mammoth could not survive in this frigid climate through one season on the scanty supply of herbage now furnished by the barren waste of Siberia,—a country, in fact, like Key West, only suitable as a habitation for exiles. I only mention this land of ice as an example, having once been blessed with a temperate climate, suited to the growth and perpetuity of the largest mammifers; whereas in our geological period, the alluvium, the largest animals are alone found in the warmest climates, where luxuriant vegetable growth perpetually abounds. Consequently, the drift period could not have occurred in the days of the patriarchs, as no record is left us, either by divine or profane historians, of so remarkable a change in the seasons or in the temperature of the globe; and in fact geology unmistakably points back to this era with evidences that cannot be gainsayed, and marks its history as antedating centuries, the primeval records of the blushing race. Referring to the fossil remains of man, the book of rocks indubitably testifies to his existence upon the earth at an epoch long preceding any historical records that we possess, if we discard the written traditions of the Hindoo and Chinese, which extend back millions of years, as alluded to in a previous page of this treatise. And at the same time we find man's remains coeval with and even buried beneath the fossil relics of extinct animals, which lay many feet under the surface, and whose existence on this globe refers back to the aboriginal races that preceded Adam many, yes, many centuries. We have the fossil remains of man taken from the alluvion of Louisiana, deposited there in all probability fifty thousand years ago,—a calculation easily made, by comparing the successive accumulations in the delta of the Nile with the delta of the Mississippi River.

The importance of the annual inundations of the Nile, not only to Egypt, but to the ancient world at large, drove the Egyptians to the necessity of erecting a Nilometer* in the valley of the Nile, which has left the accurate rise of water for two thousand years; and not only have we the rise of water noted, but the actual deposit of earth for thousands of years. For instance, the depth of soil around the base of the colossal statue of Memnon at Thebes gives us an accumulation of sedimentary deposit of less than four inches for a century; other observations in the valley of the Nile, however, give an accumulation of five inches to the century. Taking this as a basis in reference to accumulations in the valley of the Mississippi, where there are much less impurities contained in the waters, we find by calculation that the augmentation of the soil would have required over fifty thousand years to elapse since these relics ceased to represent active human life; and in addition thereto, they correspond in form and configuration with the aborigines of America. Likewise do the relics taken from the vicinity of Natchez, in the State of Mississippi, underlying a diluvial deposit of consider-

* An instrument for measuring the rise of water during the floods.

able depth, and found imbedded several feet beneath the fossil remains of the extinct megalonyx,—one of the large mammifers and allied to the sloth in form. Man fossilized most assuredly has been found in France, England, Germany, Spain, Canada, in the valley of the Mississippi, in Brazil, and in the mountain caverns of the Alps and Apennines. And wherever found in caves, his bones are closely associated with broken pottery and the relics of his faithful dog, showing the remarkable attachment which the canine in every age has had for his master, whether that protector was Indian, Chinese, or Caucasian.

And as a further proof, in America man's relics are mingled with fossilized bones of the horse long since extinct. They had both perished by some general convulsion of nature which man in this country survived, or others came in after-ages and took his place amid the fertile vales and inviting slopes of this newly-discovered hemisphere; while every reader remembers that when Columbus first anchored his bark in the haven of the New World no horse was found, nor did the tradition of the natives give rise to even a faint supposition of any former knowledge of this noble animal. During the glacial period there are no evidences that the human family had an existence upon the earth, as no traces of art have been discovered during this or any preceding period that would indicate that he as yet moved and had a being. But at a later era we found him as a savage, under the name of troglodyte, dwelling not in houses, but in the caverns of the earth, and securing his daily food by pursuit of the wild animals of the forest, and his only weapon of attack a rudely-constructed bow which projects an arrow pointed with the rough-chipped flint,—the first work of art accredited to man in his primitive savage state. Specimens of this rude architecture used in the aggressive and defensive warfare of nature's first savages have been found in America in many States of the Union, buried deeply in the bosom of the earth. And in England and on the continent of Europe the fossil remains of men abound in the ossiferous caves, commingled with those of the dog, wolf, fox, elephant, mammoth, and other extinct animals with which he contended in the chase, and which were required for his use both as respects food and raiment,—a more than ordinary hypothesis that he was cotemporary with the woolly rhinoceros, cave-bear, and the mastodon, and other extinct species of the post-pliocene period.

The autocthones, or early inhabitants of the world, were savage in their nature and unskilled in the arts of agriculture and commerce, and depended for a living upon the uncertain supply yielded in the chase and upon the spontaneous products of nature,—a system of dependence strictly adhered to at this period by the same classes of the human family who are now occupying Central and Southern Africa, Polynesia, and the uncultivated territories of North and South America. Whereas when the Adamite assumed control of his allotted hemisphere, God placed him there *to dress and tend* the garden of Eden; and when our first parents went forth condemned, the curse or command followed them, that "in the sweat of thy face shalt thou eat bread, till thou return unto the ground." The

Adamite and his descendants have ever adhered to this fiat of Heaven, and have always been emphatically an agricultural and a commercial people. In fact, husbandry is the handmaiden of civilization and enlightenment, and pursuits of the chase and a dependence upon the spontaneous products of the earth are ever the characteristic traits of the nude and barbarous of all nations and tongues.

The researches of geologists in the north of Europe have brought to light important truths connected with the prehistoric age in this portion of terra firma. In Denmark are beds of peat varying in depth from twenty to thirty feet. At the lowest depths of these bogs are imbedded pine logs, measuring three feet in diameter, and in the removal of this deposit have been found polished arrow-points of stone and other implements of a like character, though rude in their construction, but quite an improvement on the chipped instruments used by man in a more savage state and at an earlier period of his existence.

Ascending higher in these beds of peat are large layers of oak timbers, which in a former age were preceded by the pine forest along the shores of the Baltic. The pine had disappeared from the face of nature, and the oak had superseded it and covered the country with its immense forests; and in the course of ages the oak again had disappeared from its wonted hills and glades and given way to magnificent forests of beech, which now exclusively occupy this portion of Europe, and, in fact, has been the prevailing growth since the days when the Roman Empire was at its zenith. The beech is found imbedded in these peat-bogs nearest to the surface, and the oak lies intermediate between the beech and the pine. In the earliest deposits are found the rude, polished, stone implements, more perfect, comparatively speaking, than the rough, chipped arrow-heads, flint knives and hatchets of the denuded savage of the ossiferous caves of Britain and of Western Europe, who was coeval with the extinct tribes of elephants and woolly rhinoceroses of the post-pliocene epoch. Ascending higher, and examining closely among the prostrate oaks of these aged peat-bogs, are brought to light the bronze shields and swords and other implements of a race of people who had advanced sufficiently in the arts as to utilize this metal for warfare and other purposes. With the Toltecans of Central America during their conquest by the Spaniards, the only metal used by them for various purposes of husbandry was copper. They were acquainted with gold and silver, but seemed to have no knowledge of iron. We are enabled to arrive at reasonable conclusions of the state of civilization of the different inhabitants of earth and the advancement made in the arts and sciences in their various periods by the relics that mother earth has preserved for our consideration. The Romans, in the days of Julius Cæsar, found bronze instruments in use among the Britons, also with the inhabitants along the western coast of Europe. In similar bogs, and in close proximity to the surface, among prostrate beech-logs, appear, for the first time, implements of iron, testifying to a new era in the race of man, which is but a reasonable conclusion, when we reflect upon the successive gradations in the progress of creation, from the zoophyte and bivalve mollusk through all the ramifications of the animal kingdom up to the elephant and mammoth, and from the Bushman and Australian to the noblest specimen of the Divine mind, the Adamite of revelation. According to Biblical chronology, only two hundred and thirty-five years had elapsed after the creation when mention is made of Tubal Cain as an instructor of every artificer in brass and iron, demonstrating the theory that the Iron Age was alone peculiar to the blushing race, and that the age of bronze, and of polished stone, and rude, chipped stone antedated periods long prior to the advent of the enlightened Caucasian.

The periods of time during which special forests of timber may occupy certain districts of country have been computed by the scientific men of our age at fifteen thousand years; at this rate of computation the peat-bogs of Denmark are comparatively aged, and contain matters for our serious reflection.

On the shores of the Baltic are found many mounds of five to ten feet in height, composed of oyster-shell, cockle, mussel, and shells of other edible salt-water fish, and interspersed through these mounds are stone implements, and remains of beasts and birds and bones of men, showing that the aborigines once lived in this region and fed upon the products of the land and the sea; and these are the only memorials they have left us of their former existence,—the refuse-heaps, the contents of which once supplied them and satisfied their demands. However, no traces of iron or bronze utensils have yet been discovered among the débris or kitchen-heaps of this ancient people; nor do there appear any of the fossil remains of the ox, horse, or sheep. These domestic animals always attend man wherever found, from the day of Adam's first departure to our day and generation. The skulls and other bones disinterred indicate small stature, with small facial angle, and seem to be allied to the Lapps and Fins of modern times. And the flesh that covered these bones was devoured alike with that which the other rubbish contributed, and furnished food for the depraved appetite of a savage and ferocious race. And the period indicated from the evidences gathered from these kitchen-heaps corresponds closely with the oldest deposits in the peat-beds. These shell-mounds, the only evidence of an extinct race, are nothing new on the American continent. Along the sea-shore of Massachusetts and Georgia, and in Southern Louisiana, near the alluvion bordering on the various lakes adjacent to the Lower Mississippi, I have seen these shells piled up in considerable mounds and dotting the landscape around for acres, which were no doubt the rubbish-heaps of the aborigines of this country at a period antedating the traditions of the surrounding Indian tribes.

In the office of Messrs. Eager & Lusk, of New Orleans, I had the pleasure of examining a skull which had been recently removed from a shell-bank in Saint Tammany Parish, at the mouth of the Tangipaha River. It was imbedded six or seven feet beneath the surface; and immediately above this relic and overspreading it stood a magnificent live-oak tree, measuring full three (3) feet in diameter,—a noble shaft for nature to erect over the denuded bones of some poor wretch who had contributed a meal to satisfy the depraved appetite of the ancient denizens of Louisiana. These memorials of the past are replete with the records of antiquity, and it behooves us who are in search of truth to study them with care, and apply them impartially to the history of the human family.

Referring to the ancient monuments left us by the aboriginal tribes of Western Europe, every impression thrust upon the mind savors of gross barbarism and extreme savageness of character. And where in the wide domain of modern research or ancient history has any nation or tribe of people emerged from darkness with any improvement of their primitive brutal instincts without assistance from some enlightened source? Not one tribe yet, amid the researches of the past, unassisted has made any improvement in the arts of civilization. And the reverse of the proposition is also true: the fair race is progressive, and does not relapse unassisted into barbarism and savage ferocity. Instances, however, may be cited where a listless inertness has assumed sway where progress and activity once prevailed. But to clothe the white man in the garb of a savage and invest his soul with every brutal instinct and warp his frame in conformity with the mould of the Hottentot and Bushman, draws heavily in this enlightened age upon the credulity of the progressive mind. With these remarks we dismiss the subject of geology and the slight allusion made as respects archæology.

CHAPTER XV.

LANGUAGE.

"I do not much dislike the matter, but the manner of his speech."
SHAKSPEARE.

As each distinct race of mankind came originally from the omnipotent hand of Jehovah, in their respective periods of creation they were endowed by the great First Cause with certain mental faculties adapted to their peculiar wants, and were not thrown out at random upon the face of earth, nor placed in latitudes unsuited to their physical organization. Vegetable and animal life abounded in the tropics in the earlier epochs of the world, and the negro took his position in Central Africa endowed with voice, utterance, and other appliances physically and mentally adapted to his crude nature,—perfect in himself, as emanating from Deity, and a shade higher in the scale of being than the quadrumana tribes of the surrounding forest. The hand that created him planted within his nature a language adapted to his requirements, and with this peculiar gift his ideas were shaped and found utterance, which formed the basis for that intercommunication of thought and expression of desire which the lower animals had never possessed to the same perfection. This expression of thought becomes language with the first bimana inhabitants of this planet. Long prior to this, however, the feathered tribes had sang their morning carol to the rising sun, and at closing twilight chirped their parting requiem to the expiring day. The brute in every age has had his voice and his language, so remarkably adapted to his peculiar wants and instincts. And He who formed them indued their nature with that peculiar utterance that marks their distinctiveness and individuality of species, wherever the utterance is made or the sound falls upon the listening ear. The lowing herd, the growling tiger, the roaring lion, and the barking dog are distinct and recognizable in every land, climate, country, and age.

The same is true of the different languages spoken by the different aboriginal races of mankind. The diversities existing between the Caucasian, the Mongol, and the negro, in color, appearance, and general physical conformation, is as palpable as reason would demand to establish a separate and distinct originality. And no less palpable is the evidence that separates the languages of the three races enumerated above, and marks them fundamentally original gifts to the present respective owners, however more or less encroached upon by an admixture, superinduced by an amalgamation of language as well as blood, among the various races at an early epoch of the world's history.

National types would never be subject to changes if there was no adulteration of blood by amalgamation; neither would languages undergo changes to the same extent unless affected by the introduction of foreign influences. The Israelite is the same to-day that he was over three thousand years ago, and as distinguishable in feature and lineament as though handed down to us in marble statuary. In this same light may we regard languages. The Basque language in France can be traced unerringly back to the Turanian stock for full three thousand years, encroached upon as it has been by the vicissitudes of relentless war, with a view of ultimate extermination. And the Coptic, which was the speech of Egypt for five thousand years, still leaves imperishable monuments of its antiquity which science traces with no erring hand. And the Chinese, peculiar to its own originality for the past five thousand years, stands forth prominent and unalterable as the law of the Medes and Persians in structure, sound, and derivation.

The following appertaining to this subject emanates from Professor Agassiz, whose views always carry weight and interest with them: "As for languages, their common structure, and even the analogy in the sounds of different languages, far from indicating a derivation of one from another, seem to us rather the necessary result of that similarity in the organs of speech which causes them naturally to produce the same sound. . . . Would not the power the American Indians have naturally to utter gutturals, which the white can hardly imitate, afford additional evidence that these races did not originate from a common stock, but are only closely allied as men, endowed equally with the same intellectual powers, the same organs of speech, the same sympathies, only developed in slightly different ways in the different races, precisely as we observe the fact between closely-allied species of the same genus among birds? . . . Why should not the different races of men have originally spoken distinct languages, as they do at present, differing in the same proportions as their organs of speech are modified? And why should not these modifications in their turn be indicative of primitive differences among them? It were giving up all induction, all power of arguing from sound premises, if the force of such evidence were to be denied."

Language being coeval with the first inhabitants of this sublunary sphere, in connection with geology must form an important basis for the establishment of the plurality of the races prior to the historical period, the only evidences in fact which can be brought to bear upon this question at this early epoch; and, as our favorite author* contends, is the only argument which can perfectly fix the identity of the early denizens of antiquity, laying aside for the present the letter and spirit of Revelation.

The similarity and likeness of words, and similarity of grammatical structure, constitute the resemblances existing among the various languages spoken by the different families of man. Languages, like words, have their roots or base from which they spring, and groups emanating from these send off their different dialects, which are always traceable back to the original stock from which they sprung; and by analogy and comparison science derives conclusions which bear testimony in unison with the voice emanating from the book of rocks.

The Indo-European, Aryan, or Iranian family of languages is denominated inflectional, and is spoken

---

* Professor Max Müller.

by the Caucasian race wherever they occupy in Europe, Asia, Africa, or America, and comprises the Sanscrit, the Greek, the Latin, Celtic, Teutonic, Slavonic, Gothic, and Persian. The striking resemblance existing in this family of languages in grammatical structure, corresponding vocabulary, and the derivation of terms applying to distinct objects in nature, shows conclusively the relationship which has always existed; approximating in fact to that relationship that obtains with the Indo-European family in complexion, feature, and formation.

The enterprising spirit of the Semitic and Japhetic inhabitants of earth, from whom the Anglo-Saxon is descended, fathers that indomitable energy which triumphs everywhere in respect to military prowess, the physical sciences, and the advancement in civilization and religion; and the Caucasian alone, in fact, possesses the language and the moral and mental stamina which has always been the basis of literature, art, science, moral and mental attainments in every age of the world.

Though the Semitic and Japhetic families have separated through many degrees of latitude or longitude, as the case may be, or have diverged and gone to different sections of the globe, yet there are unmistakable evidences that their languages were originally one and the same, as the words in each language expressive of relationship, or of the simple objects that meet the eye in nature, have the same words expressive of the same objects; and the linguistic affinities and resemblances are identical in grammatical structure, both in the declension of the noun and in the conjugation of the verbs, while the base or root remains fixed and unchanged through all the vicissitudes of time, place, and surrounding influences; for instance, we have in the various tongues :

English.	Greek.	Latin.	German.	Sanscrit.
Father.	*Πατήρ.*	Pater.	Fäder.	Pitri.
Mother.	*Μήτηρ.*	Mater.	Moder.	Matri.
Sow.	*Συς.*	Sus.	Sû.	Sûkara.
Mouse.	*Μυς.*	Mus.	Maus.	Mûshika.

There can be no doubt of the unity of the Caucasian languages; every philologist readily acknowledges a patriarchal origin, and all of the branches of this same language, after the dispersion, must necessarily in time have undergone many changes by the addition of other words, as the wants and the intellectual progress of the diversified families required. Still, there is an identity and distinctness in all the fundamental arrangements of the Aryan language, which stand forth audibly clear and visible to the scientific explorer. And this marked originality of language possessed by this race is replete with that perfection, as a whole, which impresses upon the reflecting mind the high and exalted origin claimed for the language of man, who was made in the image and likeness of his Divine progenitor. "The Lord God formed every beast of the field, and every fowl of the air; and brought them unto Adam to see what he would call them : and whatsoever Adam called every living creature, that was the name thereof. And Adam gave names to all cattle, and to the fowl of the air, and to every beast of the field."*

---

* Genesis ii. 19, 20.

Adam became endowed by the fiat of the Almighty with utterance, and with a vocabulary of words commensurate with the exalted position that he and his posterity were to take in the grand drama of life. He was made pure and holy in the image of his divine Master, impressed with an immortality extending through eternity, and from whose loins would spring Abraham, the father of God's chosen people, and in whose veins would flow the blood of Eloehim's Lamb, which was to be for the healing of the nations. Is it strange, then, that Adam should be endowed with a language adequate to the great ends for which he was created, and adapted to the progressive capacity of the most enlightened race in all the ramifications of science, literature, art, and commerce?

The Iranian, or Caucasian, family of languages is the only one that possesses a grammatical or organic structure, is perfect and more complete in all its arrangements, and by comparison is more modern in its date, having originated with the Adamite, the last crowning work or cap-stone in the great creative achievements of Deity.

The Turanian, or Mongolian, language is spoken exclusively by this large family of nations wherever dispersed throughout the globe. Central and Eastern Asia is the home of this language; but wherever emigration has led this people forth, or circumstances have driven them, they have still retained the fundamental rudiments of this language, which untold ages have not entirely obliterated by the admixture even of other tongues; and we find it still prevalent with the Finns and Lapps on the north of Europe; with the Basques in the Pyrenees Mountains, the Magyars of Hungary, and the Esquimaux of North America. This language, in its unadulterated state, is monosyllabic in character throughout, and is written and spoken without the assistance of grammar, and whatever of sense is derived from the use of words is expressed by accentuation and position; and, by way of illustration, a change of tone and emphasis as used by a speaker in our language, in the Turanian produces different words and gives entirely a different meaning in the conveyance of thought. Declensions, cases, and numbers, as given to persons or objects in nature in the Iranian language, and conjugations, moods, and tenses to verbs, as used by us, are entirely unknown and unused in this primitive tongue, exemplifying the previous suggestion that the language of the Mongol is distinct in all of its elements and is original in its character, and belongs properly to an age far antecedent to the Adamite, and is the exclusive property of a race of people whose ruder nature in primeval ages was better adapted to this mode of expression than the fairer and more enlightened race who succeeded them centuries subsequently as inhabitants of this already peopled globe.

In the Turanian language the root never undergoes any change, but retains its distinctness, and is isolated and visible in all of the divisions and subdivisions of its branches. We find, however, slight modifications of this rule in other languages belonging to the same stock, which have undergone changes, and must continue to do so, as an admixture takes place and the dialect of one tribe is thrust upon another by the violence of war or from commercial intercourse. And, as the Mongolian has accepted companionship, or been overrun and subdued by the Caucasian, since the days that Cain the first murderer took up his abode in their midst, we may reasonably suppose that an infusion of superior blood and superior intelligence would have its tendency to improve the language and manners of this people, and elevate them in the scale of being, and give them that apparent spirit of progress which their government and architectural records would indicate that they at one period possessed, showing their reasonable mental superiority over the Malay, Indian, and Negro.

The Caucasian, or Iranian, family of languages is denominated inflectional, because it admits of a declension of nouns, the declension and comparison of adjectives, and the conjugation of verbs, and has always been the property of the white man ; and in no instance is it upon record that this language has been used by any of the Turanian or other families of mankind.

This language is perfectly distinct in its character from any and every language spoken upon the habitable globe, and has ever been exclusively used by the descendants of the Adamite. Whereas the Turanian stock of languages is terminational and agglutinized and monosyllabic in character, inorganic and destitute of grammatical structure, and is identified wherever met with throughout the expanse of nature, and is truly the exclusive property of the Mongolian ; and in no instance within the history of our age is this stock of languages spoken by any people save those who occupy to-day Mongolian territory, or whose history, such as the Magyar, the Basque, and the Turk, can be traced back to the same original family, and whose many other traits portray characteristics of a common origin. Color, stature, mind, cranial conformation, intellectual progress, and civilization, all combine to prove identity, and establish lines of demarkation between the living races, not less obvious than the lines interlying the stratified and unstratified beds of which mother earth is composed.

We read these facts and give the palm of victory to the researches of science in the mineral world, and why not in the physical world accept man as we find him located in his present allotted sphere, distinct in color, physical formation, and in all the attributes of his nature, separate in creation and separate in origin?

I would not by sophistry or any other ungenerous mode of reasoning willfully drag down my fellow-mortal from the high position which we occupy as the intellectual leaders of mankind to the disgraceful level of the spawn of earth, as is exhibited in the Bushman, Kaffir, or Hottentot of Southern Africa. Nor can reason, religion, or duty prevail with the reflecting mind to lift up to the standard of God's noblest work the degraded African or South Sea Islander, whose physical deformity and cranial contortions are inimical to beauty and at variance to the symmetrical proportions of Heaven's crowning work, man in the image of his Maker.

The Turanian stock of languages is the oldest, and, by illustration, is spoken as a child would speak, whose expressions of desire are uttered in nouns, leaving the connections to be filled up and completed by the hearer. And the Iranian language being a more perfect is also a more modern language, and emanated direct from Jehovah, a special gift to his chosen people, and by which his oracles were to be transmitted to future ages for the benefit of future generations. Nor is it to be forgotten that Adam conversed with his Maker many years before and after this unfortunate pair had tasted the first sorrows that embittered their earthly career.

In reference to the languages spoken by the inferior races of man, the Indian, Malay, and Negro, enough is known to ascribe to each a purely monosyllabic character, without the least grammatical construction, crude in its nature and exclusively adapted to beings who are savages by nature, and whose aspirations are groveling at best, and satiable alone in the gratification of the brutal instincts of depraved humanity. There can in reality exist but minor differences among the languages of the barbarous and primeval races of men, whatever may be their cast or character, unendowed with the mental faculties that ennoble his being, frame his literature, shape his laws, and establish his government upon the immutable principles of right and equity. And where a gleam of light portrays, among these pre-adamic races, monumental records of architectural and intellectual skill, we invariably find that the Caucasian admixture of blood and brains has infused new life and genius into the aboriginal races,—while at the same time the Adamic family has suffered loss, and most assuredly has violated one of Heaven's immutable laws, and entailed upon his race a curse which a thousand generations will be unable to wipe out. It is remarkably strange, if the inferior races are descended from Adam, they must necessarily furnish indications of being more modern in every respect than we now find them,—having carried with them from their native homestead some semblance at least of the language, manners, customs, and habits of their original progenitor. Time and again they would have sat by the patriarchal tent before leaving forever the land of their forefathers, and would have conversed together touching the great deluge, which had submerged their former homes and depopulated the land which they had jointly occupied. They would have talked of Jehovah, who planted the garden of Eden and placed in its midst their first parents to tend the same. They would have known the language of their ancestors, and would have remembered the manners and customs of their primitive parents, and by no means have forgotten the fair and ruddy complexions that once gave beauty and lustre to the noble ancestors with whom they were connected by the lineal ties of consanguinity. And it is passing strange that no tradition is extant among these inferior races of the Noachic deluge and the terrible results ensuing therefrom. They could realize no god in all their calendar of worship, save in the sun, whose burning rays brought light and heat, or in the viper or beast that crawled in the shamble or loitered in the jungle. There is no tradition extant of the manners and customs, or a vestige left of the noble language inherited by the Adamic race. Nor does the thought enter his savage breast that his distorted features, elongated cranium, and dark visage emanated from the ruddy blushing race, which alone possesses the language of literature and the progressive elements of intellectuality, the mother of the arts, sciences, government, and religion.

These nude tribes have their traditions, however, and it is the same from the Andes of South America to the Himalayan Range, where the wandering white man, the child of the sun, made his appearance in their midst, clothed with the effulgence of immortal light, and before whom the dark-visaged and superstitious races bowed with humble adoration, and paid homage to the superior intelligence incased in this new importation from the Celestial land ; and, like Minerva, he stands before them, the embodiment of wisdom, and from whom they drink in those floods of light in architecture and other evidences of civilization that mark the apparent progress of the Toltecan and the other Mongolian tribes.

CHAPTER XVI.

THE ISRAELITES.

> "Yet in that generous cause, forever strong,
> The Patriot's virtue and the Poet's song,
> Still, as the tide of ages rolls away,
> Shall charm the world, unconscious of decay."
>
> CAMPBELL.

THE Negro and the Mongol have been distinctly depicted on the monuments of Egypt for over 3000 years B.C., and the identity of race is so clearly marked at this early period "that a wayfaring man, though a fool, may not err therein." And this simple fact alone bears so strongly in favor of our theory of a diversity and plurality of the races of the genus homo, that it behooves us to present in this work the history and identity of the Israelitish race, since the days when God chose them from the rest of mankind to become his peculiar people. As Adam, of all other races, was his chosen race, being alone created in his own image and likeness, so, also, was Abraham selected in preference to all other families of the Adamites to become the progenitor of his chosen people. Gen. xii. 1–2: "Now the Lord had said unto Abram, Get thee out of thy country, and from thy kindred, and from thy father's house, unto a land that I will shew thee: and I will make of thee a great nation."

This message was delivered to Abraham 1921 years B.C., according to Ussher; and the Lord showed him the land of Canaan and said, "Unto thee and thy seed will I give this land." The following year there was a grievous famine in the land of Canaan, and Abram went down into Egypt to sojourn there during the reign of Salatis, or Saites, the first king of the fifteenth dynasty, 2080 years B.C. by Egyptian chronology. And after having remained in Egypt two years, he returned to Canaan again, enriched by Pharaoh's liberality, and called on the name of the Lord. In the course of a very few years Abram became very much embarrassed by the scantiness of pasturage and the increasing confusion engendered between his herdsmen and those of his nephew Lot, when, by mutual consent, Lot retired with his herds to the valley of the Jordan, and made his abode in Sodom, one of the cities of the plain. And at no distant day we find Abram taking up arms, he and the male portion of his household, with his Amorite allies, and pursuing the Chaldean monarch, who was returning to his own country laden with the spoils taken from Abram's nephew, Lot, and the neighboring Canaanites. And Abraham proved himself no ordinary champion on the field of battle, and returned home in triumph, a proud victor over the allied forces of the Chaldean monarch. And this same spirit of genius that shed such lustre around the brow of the Hebrew father at this early period is only an index of the giant mind displayed by this people even in our day in any sphere of life where talent or taste may direct their energies, of which we shall speak in its proper place.

Ten years after his return to Canaan, still being childless, at the request of his wife he took the Egyptian maid Hagar, whom he had brought out of the land of the Pharaohs, and she became his concubine; and her son Ishmael became the father of the nomad Arabs of ancient and modern history, and it was declared by Heaven "that he should be a wild man, and that his hand should be against every man, and every man's hand against him." It is, however, through Isaac and his posterity that we look for the Hebrews. According to Biblical chronology, in the year 1729 B.C. a band of Ishmaelites in passing through Canaan purchased Joseph of his brethren for twenty pieces of silver, and carried him down to Egypt and sold him to Potiphar, an officer of Pharaoh's, and captain of the guard. Twenty-four years after Joseph's arrival Jacob came down to Egypt with all of his family, numbering ninety Hebrews, and settled in the land of Goshen. Joseph, it is well remembered, at this epoch was prime minister of

Pharaoh, that is, of Assa (according to the computations of Mr. Poole), who was the fourth successor of Salatis, one of the kings of Egypt, as found on the hieroglyphics of Memphis, about 2080 B.C. according to Egyptian chronology, which differs materially from that of Archbishop Ussher.

Joseph, being in a strange land and among a strange people, married a woman of the country, who was the daughter of the priest of On, and no doubt devoted to the idolatrous worship practiced by the entire inhabitants of the land. Joseph had already been promoted from prison life to the exalted position of the prime minister to the first monarch of the earth, and was pleased to remain in his newly-adopted country, foreseeing, by the inspiration of the Divine Spirit, the impending famine, which his foresight and extraordinary wisdom amply provided for;* and there are many reasons to believe that this Pharaoh and his court became the worshipers of the true God. But in the course of time there arose a "new king who knew not Joseph." And this king was Amos, or Amosis,† of profane history, and called by Josephus Tethmosis, who was the first king of the eighteenth dynasty, about 1525 years B.C.; and, according to the best testimony, Amosis, the representative of the Theban dynasty, overthrew the Memphian Pharaohs,

---

* And besides, there was a memorable prophecy uttered by Heaven itself, which had its bearing upon the son of Jacob: "But in the fourth generation the Hebrews shall again return to Canaan. For the iniquities of the Amorites is not yet full." The fiat had gone forth, and the decree of destiny must await its literal fulfillment.

† Rameses, a line of kings.

who were the shepherd kings of Egypt and the former friends of the Hebrew children. When the Theban dynasty became a fixture in this portion of Egypt, the Israelites were looked upon as the natural enemies of the present conquerors; and lest they should unite with the remaining inhabitants to throw off the yoke of the oppressor, they were enslaved, and grievous burdens were entailed upon this unfortunate race. And, with a view of exterminating this people, a decree went out from the Theban monarch that all the males of the children of Israel should be surreptitiously disposed of at their birth, as this chosen people were already numerous, and were daily increasing the apprehensions of the reigning dynasty. An exposed infant was found by Pharaoh's daughter while she and her maidens were bathing in the waters of the Nile. It was floating by the brink of the stream in an ark of bulrushes. The daughter of Amosis, being moved with pity, had the infant Moses carried to her father's palace, and, like Joseph, he became a deliverer to this downtrodden and afflicted people. Moses at an early age took a deep interest in the affairs of the overtasked Hebrews, which interference brought upon him the threatened vengeance of his adopted father, the sovereign of the land. And for safety Moses fled to Midian, where he sojourned some time, and married Zipporah, the daughter of Jethro, the priest of Midian, and who was a lineal descendant of Abraham by his Arab wife, Keturah.

The length of time which the Israelites must certainly have endured these hardships under the Rameses kings involved a period of eighty to a hundred years.

Moses fed the flocks of his father-in-law during forty years in the land of Midian, when Jehovah, in the silent recesses of the desert of Mount Sinai, at the mount of God, presented himself face to face to Moses, and commissioned him to lead forth the Israelites from the land of bondage to that better land of Canaan, which was then flowing with milk and honey and ready to receive the long-absent exiles.

The iniquities of the Amorites at this period was no doubt full, and Moses went forth in the discharge of this duty, assisted by his brother Aaron; and the demand was made upon the king of Egypt that the people might repair to the wilderness to keep a feast in honor of their God Jehovah. The obstinate determination of this monarch, however, brought death into every household in the land of Egypt, save where the blood of the paschal lamb upon the lintels of the doors guided the angel of death in his march of destruction. And the Passover now celebrated by this people is an emblem of that mercy vouchsafed on this memorable occasion.

The Exodus commenced at Ramesis, in the vicinity of Heliopolis, during the eighteenth dynasty, under the reign of Menptah, the son of Rameses II.; and the Israelites went out under the protection of Jehovah, guided by a pillar of cloud by day and a pillar of fire by night, to whom he gave laws for their government, and confided to their keeping those great truths which were to be preserved for the benefit of the human family. And to this much-abused and persecuted race are we indebted for the revealed will of God, as presented to us in the law and the prophets.

When Jacob died in Egypt, we are told by the sacred writer that his body was embalmed by the physician, and Joseph and his brethren, after seventy days, carried his remains to Canaan and buried them in the cave that is in the field of Machpelah, which Abraham bought for a burying-place of Ephron the Hittite, before Mamre. So was Joseph's body embalmed after his death, and his bones were carried by his brethren and buried at the same place. And with these lights before us, are we astonished to find in our day the embalmed relics of the ancient Jews in a perfect state of preservation in the monuments of Egypt.

At an early day, as respects the history of this people, it is true that there was an admixture of other families of the Adamic race. Joseph married an Egyptian woman, and Moses wedded a Midianite; and later still, Solomon took wives from among the Moabites, Amorites, Hittites, etc., and also married a daughter of the Egyptian king Sheshonk, of the twenty-first dynasty, 1085 years B.C. These slight adulterations were soon absorbed, and made no impression upon their national character; for in every age and in every clime the physical characteristics of this race were as distinctly marked as is observed in the present age and in our own country, or where they have wandered off and been dispersed as captives, or lost their records and violated the commands of Heaven by intermarriages with other races.

There are instances where they have amalgamated with the inferior races, and their complexions and physical characteristics have undergone material changes, as is the case with the black Jews, so called, of Malabar, whose blood has been dreadfully adulterated with Mongolian and Malayan admixture. Dr. Buchanan, who has given this subject considerable attention, says "their Hindoo complexion, and their very imperfect resemblance to the European Jews, indicates that they have been detached from the present stock in Judea many ages before the Jews in the West, and that there have been intermarriages with families not Israelitish. . . . The white Jews look upon the black Jews as an inferior race, and as not of *pure caste*, which plainly demonstrates that they do not spring from a common stock in India." Therefore it would be absurd to advance the theory that the complexion and physical configuration of this people had been superinduced by climatic influences, and consequently the white man may degenerate and finally assume the hideous proportions of the Bushman, Australian, or Fuegean. Such is not in unison with the past records of the Jewish race.

Though war, famine, pestilence, persecution, and dispersion have attended this people for thousands of ages, and have driven them from their early habitations and associations; and the world, though divided in other respects, seems to have been united in the work of extermination, and to have clothed them with the curses and maledictions of fiendish animosity, as though acting in conformity with the behests of Divine revelation; the world ever destitute of the milk of human kindness and forgetful of that charity which brings solace to the wanderer from the homestead of childhood; amidst all these changes and vicissitudes, wherever the Jewish race is found dispersed through the habitable globe, we find that same unvarying permanence of type which distinguishes the descendants of Abraham from all other known races of man. The same features prevail in the land of Mesopotamia, where once was the seat of their glory and prosperity; the same predominates whether as aliens scattered over Western or Southern Asia, in Africa, Europe, or America. Go where you will, on the elevated plains of Central Asia, along the caravan routes through Oriental deserts, amid the isles of the sea, in the marts of the Old or the New World, we find the Jew possessing the same Hebrew lineaments that characterized the chosen few that emigrated to Egypt at the bidding of Joseph, then acting as prime minister of Pharaoh. And if at any period they have lost their distinguishing features, it was because of amalgamation with inferior races both in point of intellect and physical formation. It should be remembered as a well-established fact that of the twelve original Hebrew tribes, only two of those tribes, Judah and Benjamin, have thus far been able to keep up and preserve their records; and they are to-day as pure and unsullied in all the characteristics of feature and peculiarities of character as when Moses led them forth through the wilderness to the land of Canaan.

In the eighth century before Christ, Arbaces, or Tiglath-Pileser, King of Assyria, carried away captive thousands of the subjects of the kingdom of Israel, who dwelt in Galilee and on the eastern side of the river Jordan; and, twenty years after this period, Salmaneser, the son of Tiglath-Pileser, conquered Samaria and put an end to the kingdom of Israel.

The work of destruction that was left undone by

these two monarchs was completed forty years afterwards by Esarhaddan. The Israelites were carried as captives and sold into slavery in the land of Media, and their homes and fields were occupied by colonies transplanted from many of the Medo-Persian provinces, who brought with them and continued the worship of their false deities, and in after-times assumed the name of Samaritans, and incorporated into their religion an admixture of Judaism and heathenism. A people every way repugnant to those Israelites who still tenaciously clung to the ceremonials of their great lawgivers.

About one hundred years later, Nebuchadnezzar overran Judea, and destroyed the first temple at Jerusalem, and returned to Babylon with many captives and ladened with a great part of the treasures of the temple. This captivity lasted seventy years, when Zerubbabel and Joshua, in company with nearly forty-three thousand souls, returned to Jerusalem and commenced the erection of the second temple, under the auspices and by the decree of the Medo-Persian monarch, Cyrus the Great, which was confirmed and carried out by his respective successors, Darius and Artaxerxes Longimanus, who, in Scripture, was called Ahasuerus, the husband of Queen Vashti. After the seventy years of captivity had expired, many of the Israelites remained in the provinces where they had been placed by the kings of Assyria and Babylon, and but few, comparatively speaking, of this race returned to their original homes, and those that gathered back were principally of the tribes of Judah and Benjamin; hence the country afterwards was called Judea, and the race at large called Jews.

A portion of each of the other tribes united with these two and became one and the same; whereas the ten lost tribes remained in their newly-adopted homes in the land of Assyria, and in time were despised and down-trodden, and were absorbed more or less by the surrounding nations; and travelers assert that to this day a marked resemblance to this people is still traceable in the Persians and Afghans of the East; though many were absorbed and lost their identity during this period of subjugation, while others are still distinct and isolated among the varied inhabitants of earth. Remarkable, but nevertheless true, wherever met with in any climate or country, we invariably recognize them as belonging to the Hebrew race. Mummied Jews have been taken from the tombs of Egypt, some of them being bitumenized, and no doubt as old as their great leader, Moses, who flourished nearly thirty-five hundred years ago, with cranial formation a fac-simile of a majority of that race, as observed frequently in this the nineteenth century. From the same source the Negro and the Turanian have been obtained painted in relievo thirty-five hundred years ago with all the characteristics of their peculiar races, proving conclusively that the white, yellow, and black races were as distinct, separate, and isolated in formation and complexion as we find them to-day in their different climates and countries.

What a commentary, then, upon the ultra views of the one-origin party! How readily, then, must this marked change have taken place in the human family after the destruction of man by the Noachic deluge! From the flood to the Exodus was only eight hundred and fifty-six years, and if Shem, Ham, and Japhet, in the division of the races, are to be regarded as the progenitors of the white, yellow, and red man, to whom, then, shall we look as the father and progenitor of the black man? Only four hundred and eighty-five years had elapsed when the confusion of tongues occurred at the Tower of Babel, and the time when the Israelites crossed the Red Sea, on their march to Canaan, yet the Mongolian and the Negro were familiar to the Egyptian before Abraham saw those vast pyramids looming up from the bosom of the Nile. If Revelation, then, be silent upon the subject of the diversity of the races, then science with the aids at her command can alone solve this question. Abraham was born in 1998 B.C., just one year after Noah's death, and it was exactly fifty-five years (Biblical chronology) after the dispersion and confusion of tongues that Abraham made his entry into Egypt, he being at this time seventy-five years old, and his wife, Sarah, sixty-five years of age. And yet at this early day after the dispersion of the human family, we find Egypt peopled with a mighty race, and Abraham a perfect stranger in their midst,* and had not God interfered in his behalf Pharaoh would have appropriated his wife, Sarah, because she was fair to look upon; but Heaven's protecting care vouchsafed to him a safe return, with numerous servants and herds of cattle.

When Abraham made his exit from Egypt, he carried with him Hagar, the Egyptian maid-servant, who became his concubine; and it is highly probable that she was a hybrid cross of the genuine Copt, or ancient

---

Gen. xii. 10–15.

Egyptian, with the Mongolian race, which very naturally accounts for the peculiar character and proclivities of the descendants of Ishmael,—nomad in disposition, and highwaymen by trade.

It is asserted that the Jew stands before us as an everlasting monument of God's displeasure. All mankind, then, unfortunately, is embraced in the same dilemma, as all have erred. But verily, he stands before us as an everlasting monument of God's perfect image and likeness, exemplified in His own Son when He took upon Himself our infirmities: perfect in stature, complete in physical organization, and unimpaired in the intellectual endowments of the genus homo as the day when he came a crowning model from the plastic hand of Jehovah Himself.

European principalities dare not wage war one against the other without first testing the financial resources of the Rothschilds, the princes of bankers. A nod of recognition or approval from these giant dispensers of material aid draws forth the obsequious smile from the royal applicant and moves forward the dreadful tramp of armed legions; or disapprobation on their part in the refusal of the sinews of war lulls the impending storm and hushes the notes of the coming strife. Wealth is power, and the Israelite knows its resources and wields this giant lever with the administrative capacity of a master-intellect, for the purpose of furthering his ends and preserving the importance and protection of his race.

The leading spirit in the British Parliament is an Israelite of no ordinary calibre. "By force of talent, industry, and perseverance, unaided by wealth or family connections, in spite of the disadvantages of his Jewish origin and his reputation of a mere novelist, he has raised himself to the position of leader of the House of Commons, and of minister of finance in the greatest commercial empire of the world." And, at the English bar, J. P. Benjamin, of American celebrity, stands without a peer; whose oratory has been listened to and admired in the halls of Congress, and whose statesmanship has been felt in all the departments of the American government.

The patriot Jew, though oppressed and persecuted by emperors and republics, by sultans and popes, we find him battling for freedom under Polish and Austrian rule in the Franco-Germanic war, and breasting the storm in the internecine struggle that drenched with blood the American soil. They have numbered their philosophers among the Saracens of the East, and have transplanted their wisdom to every land where toleration would admit a ray of light. And wherever a spirit of liberty has actuated the nationalities of earth in extending to this oppressed people the exalted privileges of citizenship and uniform equality of rights, we find that they soon take that position in society and in the national councils which worth of character and force of intellect in every age have attained, illustrating peremptorily the undiminished and progressive mental capacity of the perfect Caucasian during the extended scale of near four thousand years.

Can we now, then, reconcile our conscience or the dictates of reason in harmonizing the theory that the degraded Bushman or the savage Fuegean is a lineal descendant of the patriarchs, and necessarily a twin-brother of the intellectual race whose history we have traced in these pages? If so, our efforts are in vain: permanent form and feature are a nullity, and intellectual progress a myth, as respects the characteristics of the blushing race.

CHAPTER XVII.

THE BATTLE OF ARMAGEDDON.

"And say, Supernal Powers, who deeply scan
Heaven's dark decrees, unfathomed yet by man,
When shall the world call down, to cleanse her shame,
That embryo spirit, yet without a name?"—CAMPBELL.

EZEK. xxxviii. 14–16: "Therefore, son of man, prophesy and say unto Gog, Thus saith the Lord God; In that day when my people of Israel dwelleth safely, shalt thou not know it? And thou shalt come from thy place out of the north parts, thou, and many people with thee, all of them riding upon horses, a great company, and a mighty army: and thou shalt come up against my people of Israel, as a cloud to cover the land; *it shall be in the latter days*, and I will bring thee against my land, that the heathen may know me, when I shall be sanctified in thee, O Gog, before their eyes."

In the latter days the spirit of prophecy has revealed

to our finite minds the great struggle which is to take place in the grand drama of this world's future history, which looms up with tenfold magnitude in the contemplation of the subject now under consideration. The time will most assuredly arrive, and the day is not far distant, when the armies of the living God and the infidel host of this world shall be gathered together in the great valley of Hamon-gog,* a place which in the Hebrew tongue is called Armageddon,† when "Satan shall be loosed out of his prison, and shall go out to deceive the nations which are in the four quarters of the earth, Gog and Magog, to gather them together to battle: the number of whom is as the sand of the sea." And the revelator John‡ declares that "I saw an angel standing in the sun; and he cried with a loud voice, saying to all the fowls that fly in the midst of heaven, Come and gather yourselves together unto the supper of the great God; that ye may eat the flesh of kings, and the flesh of captains, and the flesh of mighty men, and the flesh of horses, and of them that sit on them."

This is to be the final struggle between the armies of Jehovah and the allied powers of darkness.

> "The Word of God§
> Clothed with a vesture dipped in blood"

will command the celestial host against Apollyon,‖ the prince of the powers that be, called in the Hebrew tongue Abaddon. And this demon of unrighteousness is the great spirit of idolatry that the Adamite encoun-

---

* Ezek. xxxix. 11. † Rev. xvi. 16. ‡ Rev. xix. 17, 21.
§ Rev. xix. 13. ‖ Rev. ix. 11.

tered when he made his advent in this world. The devil, with his rebellious followers, "which kept not their first estate, but left their own habitation, the Lord hath reserved in everlasting chains under darkness unto the judgment of the great day." They were cast out of heaven, and in retaliation against the great Father of Light commenced their warfare against the pre-adamite until the last mortal surrendered himself, a willing subject to the powers of perdition. And throughout the vast area of earth there was not a soul but what willingly bent the knee to worship at the shrine of Baal. The creature man then stood before Jehovah as an outcast, the foe of Heaven, and the enemy of righteousness, with no hope of return until the cup of his iniquity was full. "And God said, Let us make man in our image, after our likeness," and Adam and Eve became living souls. And the serpent appeared to our first parent in the form and type of the true Mongolian, clothed with the habiliments of the artful deceiver, with the twofold intention of dragging down the new-born race to his disgraceful level and satiating his hellish appetite upon his unwary victim.

In obedience to my knowledge of the Bible, the arch-enemy of man has never visibly appeared and held personal converse with the sons of men. He has led man on by wily machinations, as an unseen enemy, until his evil purposes were accomplished and the individual has become tributary to his exactions. Satan has, however, ventured to converse with God, as reported in Job's history, and he has cried out to the Son of God when being ejected from the unhappy lunatic who made his abode in the tombs. Also he tempted

Christ during his sojourn in the wilderness, and has dared to dispute with our Saviour and the angel Gabriel. With man, however, he has never held personal interviews in the form and attitude of a being possessing material substance. But in the fulfillment of this prophecy, the time is not far distant when he is to marshal his clans for the great battle of Armageddon. Listen to the word of inspiration. Rev. xvi. 12–14: "And the sixth angel poured out his vial upon the great river Euphrates; and the water thereof was dried up, that the way of the kings of the east might be prepared. And I saw three unclean spirits like frogs come out of the mouth of the dragon, and out of the mouth of the beast, and out of the mouth of the false prophet. For they are the spirits of devils, working miracles, which go forth unto the kings of the earth and of the whole world, to gather them to the battle of that great day of God Almighty." The unclean spirit emanating from the mouth of the dragon is the archangel of darkness; and the unclean spirit from the mouth of the beast is the creature, the pre-adamic antichrist, and the other unclean spirit is Mahomet, the false prophet of Islamism. United under one banner, and with but one object to accomplish,—the overthrow of the Christion religion,—undivided they will march in their work of destruction, and the way will be opened by the angel of the Apocalypse, who will pour out his vial of wrath upon the great river Euphrates, to dry up the waters, that the way of the kings of the earth might be prepared. In other words, the Lord of Sabaoth will open up a way in due time for the concentration of the mighty forces which are to be arrayed against the Lion of the Tribe of Judah in anticipation of the great victory, when the Lamb of God shall be once more and forever crowned the "King of kings and Lord of lords."

Magog was originally a son of Japhet, and the prophet Ezekiel unites with Magog and Gog both Gomer and the house of Togarmah. The close proximity of the white race to the Turanian, and the amalgamation of races which soon ensued in the antediluvian age, brought upon the Adamite summary destruction. Nor was the posterity of Noah sufficiently mindful of this great calamity and of its great first cause to deter them from a repetition of the same offense. So we may reasonably observe, in after-ages, that Magog, Gomer, and others of the fair-complexioned race united their destiny with the Mongolian tribes of Central Asia, infused into them a higher cast of intellect, and more of the progressive spirit of the white man, and modified the feature and form of the inferior race, which has produced the varied diversity in the Turanian family, admissible wherever found scattered in their various localities, as Calmucks, Tartars, Samoyedes, Ugrians, Basques, or Lapps. This progressive spirit developed itself several centuries before the Christian era in Eastern Asia by the infusion of greater mental capacity into the inert mind of the Turanian, as we see exemplified in the structure of the Chinese wall and other architectural works of a national character found among the Chinese. History* informs us that the

* Cuneiform inscriptions. The information gained for history from the deciphering of the Assyrian sphenograms is a matter of consider-

Mongolian* was mixed at an early day with the Chaldean, owing to their proximity and the intercourse engendered by commercial relations, and brought about by the aggressive disposition of the Adamite in every age. Babylon of old has the reputation of being the first of all idolatrous cities, and stands forth in the Apocalypse as the prominent emblem of that enormous guilt which must culminate at some day and break upon the head of the idolatrous races. This nation, bordering closely on the Turanian group, instilled into the inferior race, lying on her east, greater intellectual endowments and more symmetrical form of person, at the same time imbibed a sufficient quantity of poison from their eastern neighbors that the religious and political economy of the Assyrian Empire became corrupt and demoralized in proportion as the Turanian family had been elevated in the scale of progress. And, like the antediluvian, great Babylon adopted the heresies and idolatrous worship of the aboriginal races, until her iniquities called forth the merited vengeance of offended Deity.

Gog and Magog represent the leading spirits of the pagan world, possessing inherently greater intellectual

---

able interest to all parties in search of truth. "It is certain that from time immemorial three peoples of different *characters and languages were living in close contact* and in various relations as to political power in the countries where sphenography was practiced. These three groups of nations are the Semitic, Aryan, and Turanian, or Scythic." (American Cyclopædia.) These inscriptions are found in abundance amid the waste ruins of those ancient cities lying between the Caspian Sea and the Persian Gulf, at one time the original boundary separating the Adamic from the inferior race on the east.

* Philip Smith's History of the World.

capacity. They are the champions selected to manipulate the Mongolian and other aboriginal hordes, combined with all the Mohammedan and other anti-Christian delusions, whom the arch-fiend of darkness, the master-spirit of the demonian elements, shall command in person; and, like an Alexander or a Napoleon, he will lead his infatuated host on, from conquest to victory, until the last armed foe shall expire, or his minions shall meet their doom and "be turned into hell with all the nations that forget God."

The Scythians of old are the people alluded to in the Holy Scriptures whom Hippocrates and Herodotus describe in personal appearance as exclusively peculiar to themselves, and entirely different from all the races of mankind with whom it has been their good fortune to meet in their intercourse with man. By these ancient historians they are represented with gross bodies and of corpulent stature, with loose and flexible joints, with flabby belly and scant hair, and in person there is a marked resemblance one to the other.

The Scythian soldier in the hour of conflict would cease from the bloody strife to drink the blood of the first victim slain in battle; and the skins and scalps of the fallen enemy were preserved as trophies by the victor; and the skulls of his mangled foes were converted into cups, and graced their rude bacchanalian boards during their annual festivals. And when death visited the royal household, they honored their king in his burial by sacrificing human beings, together with such animals as their flocks afforded. Their slaves they treated as brutes, and invariably put out all their eyes. Their intercourse with foreigners on terms of friendship was very limited, and foreign customs and habits were inadmissible under any and all circumstances. This aversion to foreign innovations is still a peculiar characteristic of the Oriental in our own day and generation.

The gypsies, a corruption of the word Egyptians, a vagabond, roving class of prowling thieves, who are infesting nearly every country under the sun, where civilization reigns, and where ignorance contributes material aid in encouraging treachery, cowardice, and cruelty. These wretches are an offshoot of the Scythian tribes of old, and have passed under various names in different countries, as Tartars or heathens, and are known at this day as Bohemians, having acquired that title as entering France first from the land of Bohemia. They have been banished from nearly every civilized kingdom of Europe, and are regarded as robbers, highwaymen, and vagrants by all who have had the privilege of testing their worthlessness. They have a language composed of scraps of words picked up hither and thither in their migrations round the world, which can be called nothing more nor less than "jargon,"—possessing no words which convey any idea of God, the human soul, or the immortality of man. Their physiognomy is Asiatic in type: complexion tawny, eyes black and piercing, hair very black, cheek-bones high and prominent, lower jaw slightly projected, and crania with small facial angle, and, like other Orientals, they are unreliable and exempt from every redeeming quality that marks the blushing race.

These vagabonds are the pioneers amid the haunts of civilization, who are ready to enlist in the grand army of aggression in its onward march to meet the chosen remnant, whose robes have been washed and made white in the blood of the Lamb. And well may the archangel of death rear his crested form in the proud attitude of a conqueror, having lorded it over God's heritage for nearly six thousand years, and swayed the iron sceptre of darkness over earth's myriads of souls until the dark domain of perdition has been peopled with the lost and ruined of every race. And the time must soon be ushered in when the marshaled hordes of earth shall be arrayed in line of battle to confront the angelic host; and as God said, "Let there be light, and there was light," in the twinkle of an eye the fiat will go forth, and the legions of Apollyon will roll back like a wave from the surf-beaten shore, and cry out in anguish for the mountains to fall on them and the hills to cover them. And the Lamb of God that was slain from the foundation of the world shall then make his second appearance, crowned in the glory of his celestial attire, to be and remain forever and ever the King of kings and the Lord of lords.

And when will be fought the great battle of Armageddon? and when will the great victory be achieved over the enemies of the Cross? When the wolf shall dwell with the lamb and the leopard shall lie down with the kid, when the suckling child shall play unharmed on the hole of the asp, and the weaned child shall put his hand with impunity on the cockatrice's den. "Here is wisdom." And no finite mind can answer this solemn question; it belongs to the mysterious records of futurity. We can, however, avail ourselves of such light as may be presented in Divine revelation for the consideration of sacred truth. David says, in Psalm xc. 4, "For a thousand years in thy sight are but as yesterday when it is past;" and again, 2 Peter iii. 8, "But, beloved, be not ignorant of this one thing, *that one day is with the Lord as a thousand years*, and a thousand years as one day." Then upon this data as a basis we proceed. The Lord was six days (or periods of time) in creating the heavens and the earth, and he rested on the seventh day and sanctified it as a day of rest. Adam commenced his labors on Monday morning, the first day of a thousand years; and now we, the transient occupants of earth in this the nineteenth century, are to-day bringing up and closing the labors of Saturday evening. From Adam to Christ was four thousand and four years, according to the computation of Archbishop Ussher, and from the birth of Christ to the present time is eighteen hundred and seventy-two years, which added together gives us a period of five thousand eight hundred and seventy-six years, leaving but one hundred and twenty-four years when the week of six days shall have passed away, and the six thousand years shall have swept across and fixed forever the destiny of man. Then comes in the Sabbath of a thousand years, the Christian's jubilee, the millennium of revelation. "Blessed and holy is he that hath part in the first resurrection." Let us be mindful that human chronology is only an assimilation to the truth, and that Archbishop Ussher was only a man and liable to err in his computation of passing ages, and the error of one hundred years or more on his part may thrust this generation into the very midst of a struggle, where hell and earth are combined to precipitate their murderous battalions on a sleeping and unsuspecting world, while the angelic host are tuning their harps in honor of the victory which must eventually place upon Jehovah's brow the golden crown and the victorious palm.

FINIS.

www.ingramcontent.com/pod-product-compliance
Lightning Source LLC
LaVergne TN
LVHW021359110826
845150LV00007B/1720

* 9 7 8 1 4 2 5 5 1 3 7 4 0 *